"The book of James (verse 5:4) says that the wages we fail to pay our workers cry out against us, and the cries of the workers reach the ears of the Lord Almighty. This book is an invitation for us to listen, with God, to the cries of those who labor."
— Shane Claiborne, Author of *The Irresistible Revolution*

"In the past, the labor movement has successfully fought for the 40-hour work week, weekends off work, the end of child labor, benefits, and protections for women and minorities. Today, we are once again reclaiming the insight that work and labor are important not only for individuals but for the well-being of our communities. This is what brings communities of labor and communities of faith together, as the authors of this book demonstrate. All can benefit from this emerging solidarity."
— John Patrick, President, Texas AFL-CIO, and Rick Levy, Secretary-Treasurer, Texas AFL-CIO

"In *Unified We Are a Force*, Joerg Rieger and Rosemarie Henkel-Rieger craft a crisp exploration of Americans' value for work and workers and dare to bring Jesus into the conversation. It is easy to push conversations on labor rights, wages, and workers to the margins; calling such talk 'liberal,' 'extreme,' or, worse, 'communist.' But that is a grave mistake. Jesus cares about work, wages, and workers' freedom from exploitation. This book shows us exactly why. What's more, these authors illuminate the call and power of deep solidarity—the kind of unity that echoes Jesus' declaration: 'When you did these things to the least of these, you did it to me.' Read this book."
— Lisa Sharon Harper, Chief Church Engagement Officer, Sojourners

W9-ABY-691

"Fifty years ago Dr. Martin Luther King, Jr., said America needed an economic stimulus plan with a bottom-up approach, not a banker-down approach. Together, we must form a grand alliance. Together, we must merge all people of goodwill. We believe labor rights and civil rights are one and the same, and you can't have one without the other. This approach must unite the issues of race and class, workers' rights and voting rights. We are all trade unionists now. We are all civil rights activists now. As it says in Isaiah 10, 'Woe to those who make unjust laws, to those who issue oppressive decrees, to deprive the poor of their rights.' We can win against extremism if we get unified! *Unified We Are a Force* is the handbook for all of us who work and are people of faith or goodwill, who believe in a moral universe, to join hands and march together."

— Rev. Dr. William J. Barber II, Author of *Forward Together*

"*Unified We Are a Force* is a striking challenge to build an alternative future. Constructed from a powerful reflection on twenty years of social struggles, Joerg and Rosemarie Rieger offer an unparalleled critique to the naturalization of inequality in general and understandings of labor and wealth production in particular. They urge religious communities to go beyond simplistic ideologies or parochial positionalities to create networks of true deep solidarities. This groundbreaking book is a must read for anyone interested in constructive theologies, interreligious conversations, sociology of grassroots movements, labor studies, and globalization, religion and politics."

— Santiago Slabodsky, Florence and Robert Kaufman Chair in Jewish Studies, Hofstra University

"Joerg and Rosemarie Rieger do a masterful job in laying out religious and labor history and philosophy along with the current state of affairs as our society continues to struggle with basic questions of justice, dignity, and respect for workers. Their clear understanding of the intimate intersection between faith and labor provokes thought and emotion as they offer a compelling call to action. The book leaves the reader not only well informed and motivated but actively probing their own faith and values for alignment with the political reality in front of them while searching for the divine light in each of us."

— Rudy López, Executive Director, Interfaith Worker Justice

"I have learned a lot from Joerg Rieger. He is on the cutting edge of how to mix good theology with activism. I was impressed that he shared such similar perspectives with social movements organizing in the grassroots—except Joerg Rieger gives it a new language and perspective as a great theologian. I might call him the movement theologian. I am excited to see him work with his partner to produce writing for movement and activism. I think the labor movement, and the fight for $15 minimum wage, could learn so much from this perspective. Sometimes we need to see our movements in dialogue with theologians to have new language and new eyes."

— Paul Engler, Cofounder, Center for the Working Poor and Author of *This Is an Uprising*

"Drawing on both ancient wisdom from faith traditions and the authors' own experiences forging solidarity among faith, labor, and community groups in Dallas, *United We Are a Force* offers a vision for the ways labor and religion can radicalize each other and transform our out-of-balance economy. This is an invaluable resource for anyone seeking to build coalition in the struggle for economic justice."
— Sarita Gupta, Executive Director, Jobs with Justice

"Whether in faith communities or worker centers, this book is necessary! Joerg and Rosemarie Rieger articulate the relationship between labor and faith at the heart of all human living. Simply, working people are the vast majority of the 99%, not the 1%. Calling upon ancient notions of justice, faith communities and labor organizations have much to offer in our similarities and differences working in deep solidarity to positively change the growing inequality gap in the U.S."
— Joan M. Martin, The William W. Rankin Associate Professor of Christian Social Ethics, Episcopal Divinity School

"Dr. Rieger and Ms. Henkel-Rieger's call to reclaim the value of work is good news for the poor. As this book makes clear, it is also critically important for all of us and for the health of our society and our world. If you want to understand how to take this truth seriously and integrate the value of work and of workers into our personal and common life, this book offers a comprehensive set of prescriptions and proscriptions. Read it!"
— Alexia Salvatierra, Coauthor of *Faith-Rooted Organizing*

"This is a most timely work on the unequal relationship between employers and the employed, the owners of capital and the working classes and the poor. In a world where policy decisions, corporate conduct, and business practices increasingly reduce the bargaining power and quality of life of working people, the pertinence of what is termed 'deep solidarity'—advocacy, activism and generosity—between all workers and people of conscience against a system that enriches a miniscule elite cannot be overstated. *Unified We Are a Force* provides an excellent exposition on the inequality inherent in the current economic environment, particularly in respect of labor. The authors furnish an extremely persuasive argument on how religion is—and not invariably—complicit in economic injustice. Joerg Rieger and Rosemarie Henkel-Rieger elegantly highlight the urgent need to reclaim the prophetic strands of our religious traditions to enrich the struggle for economic justice—and in the process we become more human. By examining how power, privilege, injustice, and unequal treatment against labor operate at the intersections of race, gender, ethnicity, and citizenship, among other things, the authors sketch out an image of God as the companion of the powerless and not the protector of powerful elites."

   — Farid Esack, President of the International
      Qur'anic Studies Association, and Department
      of Religion Studies chair at the University of
      Johannesburg

UNIFIED WE ARE A FORCE

HOW FAITH AND LABOR CAN
OVERCOME AMERICA'S INEQUALITIES

JOERG RIEGER AND
ROSEMARIE HENKEL-RIEGER

CHALICE
PRESS

ST. LOUIS, MISSOURI

Bible quotations, unless otherwise marked, are from the *New Revised Standard Version Bible,* copyright 1989, Division of Christian Education of the National Council of the Churches of Christ in the United States of America. Used by permission. All rights reserved.

Cover design: Jesse Turri

ChalicePress.com

Print: 9780827238589
EPUB: 9780827238596   EPDF: 9780827238602

Library of Congress Cataloging-in-Publication Data

Names: Rieger, Joerg, author. | Henkel-Rieger, Rosemarie, author.
Title: Unified we are a force : How faith and labor can overcome America's inequalities / by Joerg Rieger and Rosemarie Henkel-Rieger.
Description: St. Louis, Missouri : Chalice Press, [2016] | Includes bibliographical references and index.
Identifiers: LCCN 2016008872 (print) | LCCN 2016012683 (ebook) | ISBN 9780827238589 (pbk. : alk. paper) | ISBN 9780827238596 (epub) | ISBN 9780827238602 (epdf)
Subjects: LCSH: Solidarity—Religious aspects—Christianity. | Work—Religious aspects—Christianity. | Labor—Religious aspects—Christianity.
Classification: LCC BT738.45 .R54 2016 (print) | LCC BT738.45 (ebook) | DDC
261.8/5--dc23
LC record available at http://lccn.loc.gov/2016008872

Printed in the USA by Linemark Printing, Inc.,
part of the (Washington) DC Local chapter DC72-C.

 5

Contents

For our daughters Helen and Annika Rieger and all those who are working in the spirit of deep solidarity.

Preface

No one and nothing is unaffected by the ever-growing disparity between the proverbial 99 percent who have to work for a living—the working majority—and the 1 percent who may also work but whose wealth and power derives from other sources. This is true not only for individuals but also for their families and communities. It is true not only for the worlds of politics and economics but also for the worlds of culture and faith. The growing disparity shapes us deeply, all the way to the core. And unfortunately, young people of the 99 percent are the most affected, as the limited standards of living their parents enjoyed are eroding at an alarming pace and no one knows how they will live in a few years.

In this book we are not complaining but searching for solutions. We are convinced that all those affected by these problems can also contribute to turning things around by what we are calling *deep solidarity*.[1] Such solidarity needs to rest on broad shoulders, drawing energy from all aspects of life, politics, economics, religion, and the realities of labor or work (terms we use interchangeably).[2]

Current debates about disparity are often limited to distribution and redistribution of wealth. These are important debates, to be sure, but they prevent us from looking at how disparity is created in the first place. Worse yet, these debates can make the debaters look as if they are asking to get something for nothing, looking for handouts, or "spreading the wealth around" that they have not earned. When young people join the fight for redistribution, they are often made to look as if they are trying to mooch off the older generations. Condemnations of greed can be even more counterproductive, as they tend to disregard the ways in which such extreme wealth is produced.

In this book, we propose a better way to approach economic disparity by taking a closer look at how wealth is produced. Instead of starting with the question of distribution, we start with the question of production: Whose work and labor do we tend to value most and for what reasons? Why is the contribution of autoworkers valued so much less than the contribution of the CEOs of their companies, for instance, despite the ever-growing productivity of the workers? The essential question is, *What is the value of the contributions of the 99 percent and who determines it?*

Production, work, and labor are, of course, not simply valued by money and benefits. Value can also be expressed in how much input people have in their work, their products, and in the governance of their workplaces. Americans in particular should ask themselves why democracy should be a matter for politics and not also in the realm of economics.

This book reflects our experiences of living in Dallas, Texas, for over twenty years. Some have called Dallas the "belly of the beast" where the disparities are greater than in most any American city and where the concerns of working people find less support than in most other places. Thirty-eight percent of Dallas children live under the poverty line, a higher percentage than in any other US city above one million residents.[3] Most of their parents go to work every day.

Nevertheless, working people in Dallas have never given up and today the influence of working people and their movements is growing again, including the Texas AFL-CIO (American Federation of Labor and the Congress of Industrial Organizations). In a city that has more churches than most other places in the world, faith communities are slow to support the causes of working people. But some are waking up to the problem. Most exciting, this support is growing not only in progressive communities of faith but also in more traditional ones, bringing confirmation of the time-honored phrase, "if you can make it here, you can make it anywhere."

For the past two decades, we have collaborated with organizations and groups around the nation and around the globe. And while peoples' situations differ, our approach has helped us start this conversation on the convergence of religion, politics, and labor in many places we could never have anticipated or imagined. And we hope to begin sharing it even more and everywhere.

The chapters of this book build on each other but also stand alone. Following an overview of the problem in chapter 1, we begin to get a bit more specific covering the various challenges faced by faith communities and in the labor field, as well as ways to incorporate deep solidarity and how to make organizing changes. Chapter 2 describes the problem of work and chapter 4 covers issues faced by people of faith. People from the world of labor and other movements will find help in chapter 5, and everyone will gain help in chapters 3 and 6, on activism and deep solidarity and on organizing, respectively.

This conversation is large and ongoing, so endnotes will contain references to further reading and where further engagement may be needed.

Acknowledgments

Many people, communities, and organizations have contributed to our understanding of the connection between religion and labor. Nina Fernando, an organizer with Clergy and Laity United for Economic Justice in Los Angeles (CLUELA) commented on an earlier draft, as did Shukry Cattan, development coordinator for the UCLA Labor Center. Professors Santiago Slabodsky and Kevin Minister also provided valuable feedback on various topics.

Many communities have contributed, including faith and labor communities in Dallas and many other places around the nation and the world. In Dallas, pastors Ed Middleton of First Community Church and Keith Stewart of Spring Creek Church have been longtime allies who also worked with the Walmart peer chaplains. North Texas Jobs with Justice and its Workers' Rights Board have been the base of our work. We are also grateful to some Dallas locals of the United Food and Commercial Workers and the Walmart workers they support, a group of Ironworkers in the process of organizing, and the members of the Progressive Reading Group that has met at our house for many years.

Among other organizations, we are grateful to Jobs with Justice (JwJ), Interfaith Worker Justice (IWJ, in particular the affiliates in Kansas and Arkansas), Clergy and Laity United for Economic Justice in Los Angeles and California (CLUELA and CLUECA), the Dallas AFL-CIO Central Labor Council and the Texas AFL-CIO. We are also grateful to various worker centers and their organizers that we visited over the years, in Asheville, North Carolina; Austin, Texas; Denver, Colorado; Springdale, Arkansas; Immokalee, Florida;

Memphis, Tennessee; Phoenix, Arizona; as well as the friends at the Salt of the Earth Labor College in Tucson, Arizona. Thanks also to the organizers of the Wild Goose Festival and to Bartimaeus Cooperative Ministries, where some of our work was presented and discussed.

Among academic institutions we owe our gratitude to the Wendland-Cook Professorship endowment at Perkins School of Theology, SMU and many other institutions where we presented part of our research, including Antioch University and the UCLA Labor Center, Claremont School of Theology, Drew University, Pacific School of Religion, Hamline University, Rust College, Starr King School for the Ministry, Syracuse University, Union Theological Seminary in New York, the University of San Francisco, the Methodist University (Universidade Metodista) in Sao Paulo, Brazil, the University of Leuven, Belgium, the University of Manchester, England, and the Institut für Theologie und Politik (ITPOL), Münster, Germany.

We also appreciate support from the Cook Foundation and from the Dykes Foundation, which put on a seminar on related topics in Houston, Texas, in the fall of 2014.[1] And, last but not least, thanks to Brad Lyons and Steve Knight of Chalice Press and to our editor Mick Silva for helping us bring this work to a wider audience.

This book was printed in a union shop and so it proudly bears a union bug, which symbolizes the spirit of this project.

Introduction

"We are all workers now."—Juan Peron, *Evita*

Most of us have grown up with the belief that we are living in a middle-class country where workers are but a minority. The truth is that 99 percent of us have to work for a living, and even the 1 percent whose income derives mainly from their investments often work. Most of us are workers in one sense or another, despite the fact that some might be able to survive a little longer than others without a paycheck. Workers are still the majority, even if one defines workers in a more technical sense as those who work for someone else and who have limited power at work and over their work; 63 percent of all Americans fall into that category and the numbers appear to be rising.[1] Even young people who are graduating from college are now more likely than ever to enter the workforce as temp workers, or as employees with little power and no benefits, if they are fortunate enough to land a job. It stands to reason that we should talk not merely of the *working-class majority* but of the *working majority*.

Even seasoned professionals, who used to be proud of their independence, increasingly find themselves treated like workers, as corporations constantly increase workload, expectations, and pressure. One of the fastest groups of contingent workers consists of professionals who are college-educated and white collar.[2] Small business people often find themselves working alongside workers, experiencing similar pressures. In any case, the gulf separating the managers of large businesses from the managers of small businesses appears to be greater than the gulf separating the managers

1

of small businesses from their workers. The test for that is what happens when Walmart or a similar large corporation comes to town and puts small businesses out of existence, hand in hand with the better-paying, more fulfilling jobs.

White collar or blue collar, salaried or waged, black or brown or white, gay or straight, male or female, professionals, business people: most of us work for a living and most of us are increasingly experiencing the pressures of work. This is why we will be talking about "deep solidarity," which puts more than 99 percent of the population in the same boat. When this is seen, our diversities can be put to positive use, enabling us to work together to overcome injustice wherever we find it. The 1 percent are not necessarily excluded: they always have the option of putting themselves on the side of the 99 percent, and some do.[3] We are not excluding them from this project, they do so themselves, and this may well be the reason why "rich people have problems too," as the popular saying goes.[4]

Can there be any doubt that religion and politics are also affected by the pressures we experience at work? After all, we spend the bulk of our waking hours working for a living, which implies that work shapes us deeply. So why are these matters so rarely addressed? The good news is that much is happening to change things. There are numerous efforts by communities of faith, unions, and other groups who are making a difference. These efforts are what inspired this book.

Why Are You Here?

All of us would benefit from pondering this question every now and then. Too often, our organizations end up merely going through the motions. This is true for all types of communities that typically start out as meaningful, inspired movements.

This question was put to us in a meeting with a group of Latino ironworkers who were considering organizing to become affiliate members of a union. The workers had every right to be suspicious: Why would we—a theologian, a community organizer, and some of our allies—want to meet with them? To discuss matters of faith? More specifically, why would theologians and religious leaders want to get involved? Why not stay with their usual constituencies in their churches, synagogues, and mosques? The workers probably assumed our presence had something to do with religious charity.

In response, Joerg summarized the reasons. While many people believe the world is shaped from the top down, and that power rests with wealthy CEOs and political leaders, many religious traditions, including Christian ones and their Jewish and Muslim relatives, know it is possible to look at the world the other way around. In the Exodus from Egypt, Moses and the Hebrew slaves found that God struggles with those who yearn for liberation. Jews, Christians, and Muslims share in these ancient traditions commemorating an escape from oppression. Similar commemorations can be found in many other traditions as well.

This shared experience of liberation bears witness to the fact that the world is best changed from the bottom to the top, not the other way round. There is greater potential for transformation when working people come together and work in deep solidarity than when a president, mayor, or corporate leaders take over without consideration of the rest of us. To the 99 percent, it often doesn't occur to us that we might be closer to these ironworkers than to the 1 percent or even to the 0.1 percent who possess most of the wealth and the power it conveys in this country. Here, with the 99 percent, is where we find not only budding social and religious movements but also evidence of the divine at work among us. This reality is part of our shared heritage and we will explore it in this book, regardless of the fact that many have given up hope that the enormous disparities of the present might come to an end.

We believe that with enough people joining in solidarity, the world can truly be changed.

This project goes beyond the usual discussion of morality and what we should and should not do according to particular ethical ideals. We want to know where the greatest sources of energy and community are and how to connect with them in deep solidarity.

Special Interest?

Whose interests is this book serving?

It is one of the most pernicious misunderstandings of our times to think that work and labor are the concern of "special interest groups." In a recent interview, a theologian and community organizer claimed that a living wage was the interest of lower-class whites, while African Americans were concerned about black lives and Latinos and Latinas were concerned about the legalization of immigration. The truth is that all of these groups and anybody else who has to work for a living has a stake in matters of work and labor. Race, ethnicity, as well as gender and sexuality, are not *separate* concerns, as each of them carries implications for work and labor; these factors do not remove the concerns of work and labor; if anything they complicate them and worsen them. Conversely, work is also a significant place where race, ethnicity, gender, and sexuality are shaped, worked out and controlled, for good or for ill.

We are not trying to argue that work is all that matters. But work does matter *to everything,* touching on all issues of life and faith. It helps neither to resolve the deadly forces of racism nor the life-and-death matters of immigration without people's ability to make a living and employ their productivity for the common good. As Martin Luther King Jr., said, shortly before he was killed in Memphis in 1968: "What does it profit a man to be able to eat at an integrated lunch counter if he doesn't earn enough money to buy a hamburger and a cup of coffee?"[5] Recall that King was supporting a strike of mostly African American sanitation workers at the time of his death. Rather than playing off against each other the various sources of oppression, what happens if we join hands, following King's example? One of the greatest African American labor leaders, A. Philip Randolph, stated in 1944 that "no greater wrong has been committed against the Negro than the denial to him of the right to work."[6] Randolph believed that without economic freedom the political freedom of the African American population would be incomplete.[7] This does not mean that we should neglect the issue of police killing black people, or other causes of contemporary movements and protest. However, the challenge to the status quo is more profound when the more deeply engrained injustices are not overlooked and included in the discussion of the more visible injustices.

The Material and Spiritual Are Connected

One way to miss the value of this discussion is to consider it merely about *material* concerns. Yet work and labor are both material and spiritual matters, as they shape us all the way to the core, impacting us from our most basic needs, all the way up to our loftiest ideals. Likewise, religion and faith are both material and spiritual matters, as their concerns always have practical implications for all of life. Work and religion or work and faith cannot be separated along purely material or spiritual lines.

Indeed, in the Abrahamic traditions, no such easy separation exists. When the apostle Paul talks about the works of the Spirit and the works of the flesh, he talks about practices that incorporate both material and spiritual: "fornication, impurity, licentiousness" and "kindness, generosity, faithfulness" (Gal. 5:19, 22) In the Jewish traditions, which influenced both Christianity and Islam, salvation is not a matter of escaping into another world but of living a full life here and now, combining what we consider material and spiritual. God's covenants with Abraham and Moses, which are recognized by Jews, Christians, and Muslims, are focused on the material well-being of people rather than on some otherworldly spiritual plane. In all of the Abrahamic religions, the material and the spiritual are inseparable, and sometimes indistinguishable.

Yet though our ancient traditions do not separate the material and the spiritual, our contemporary world often does. One of the most common complaints we hear today is that people are "too materialistic." This means, supposedly, that people only care about things and how to get more things. While on the surface this sentiment appears true enough, it is wrongheaded on almost all counts.

What people really care about is not things but what these things *stand for.* The pleasure of owning a cell phone, for instance, is not primarily in the material object that it is. It is not even about owning a powerful mini computer that fits in our pockets. The pleasure in owning a cell phone comes from the power of having one's voice heard ("Can you hear me now?"), and the facilitation of our relationships to others (both those on the other end of the phone and the ones who see us using it). And ultimately, owning this material object is all about being included, admired, and loved.

Similarly with cars, houses, boats, clothing, jewelry or anything people purchase at shopping malls: what really matters is whether they are able to bring us love, keep us safe, grant us status, and function as fulfillments of our innermost desires. The most successful advertising campaigns are those that manage to establish this connection between a thing and the deeper powers it grants us and allows us to wield.

What would be the alternative to being "too materialistic?" When the problem is formulated in this way, even nonreligious people often assume the required antidote is to become "more spiritual" somehow.[8] Here, spiritual is understood as the opposite of material. Yet who says the material has to be discounted in this way? The Abrahamic traditions make us rethink this artificial division, our zero-sum game that's become too simplistic and misleading. Being human, we cannot leave the material world behind, as survival depends on food, shelter, and clothing, and other materials such as clean water and health care and physical work in some form or fashion. So why play our material reality off against some immaterial spirituality?

Jesus spoke of spirituality being tied to material reality. He said the goal is not to exchange the material for the spiritual but to exchange a broken material reality for a new one. Instead of blaming the sick (as in "Who sinned?" in John 9:2), Jesus healed the sick. Instead of condemning the poor to poverty and preaching salvation in the next world, Jesus proclaimed good news here and now (Matt. 11:5; Luke 4:18). Instead of telling the rich young ruler that his material possessions did not matter, Jesus called for him to distribute them to the poor (Mark 10:17–22). What is spiritual to Jesus is not immaterial reality but what contributes to changing an oppressive material reality into a liberated material reality.

This is the deeper implication we've tried to capture in this book. Without the reality of work and labor, any effort to talk about spirituality is in vain. And without the real possibility of transforming material reality, both labor and religion would be a waste of time.

Basic Issues

Work and Labor: Why Should Anybody Care?

Despite the fact that "hard work" is still officially considered the way to success and that virtually all of us have to work for a living, work and labor matter surprisingly little these days. This is true in almost all areas of life, including economics, politics, and even religion. Moreover, this is true across the ideological spectrum, with few exceptions.

In the worlds of economics and business, the focus is on portfolios and the value of stocks rather than on work and workers. Both the law and the prevalent business logic dictate that the interest of stockholders trumps the interest of workers. The value of companies is decided on the basis of profit with little regard for the treatment or the happiness of workers. The business pages of the newspapers may report economic productivity gains in broad strokes but rarely report what is happening at the workplace either. In our experience, the media often refuse to cover problems and abuses at the workplace even when these matters are brought to their attention by esteemed representatives of the community. Yet what if economics is not primarily about money and stocks but about work, who does it, how it gets done, and who benefits from it?[1]

In the world of politics and power the focus is on those who can finance campaigns and who belong to the networks of power that are able to determine what is to be done, rather than on those whose work and whose taxes make politics possible. Elections are won by talking about wedge issues like religion, guns, and sexuality. Campaigns rarely include the topic of work, and even the more progressive politicians are, for the most part, surprisingly silent on the topic. In addition, hundreds of thousands if not millions of working people are actively kept away from the polls by Voter ID laws and other hurdles such as long lines at the polls in minority neighborhoods, spread of misinformation, and sometimes even intimidation. As a result, many working people are deprived of a major part of their ability to participate in democratic politics. What if politics is not primarily about elected leaders but about the ones who elect them, the 99 percent who work for a living, the working majority?

Not even in the world of religion does work matter much, as the focus of religious communities is mostly on what happens during leisure time and on religious performances that take place when people are not at work.[2] Those who attend worship services are not only off work but are often trying to forget about work. It should not surprise us that much of religion is more interested in what happens in the bedroom than what goes on in the boardroom and that it seems even less interested in other places where people work. Sometimes religion assumes that its task is to regenerate people on their days off work for whatever it is they need to do back at work, but even in this case there is little concern for what really happens at work let alone for transforming what happens at work. What if religion is not primarily about what happens in another dimension but about what difference the divine and people of faith are making in this world, including what happens at work?

The most fashionable positions across the ideological spectrum also seem to be at a loss when it comes to the topic of work. Conservatives of all colors emphasize the value of hard work, but when it comes to actual work they are quick to blame those who do it. Those who have trouble making ends meet financially are blamed for being lazy or are considered unworthy of adequate pay, no matter how hard they work. Even working more than one job at a time, as many low-wage workers are forced to do, does not seem to be enough. The multitude of liberals care about many injustices, paying attention to matters of gender, sexuality, race, ethnicity, the environment, and even poverty, but there is surprisingly little engagement of issues having to do with work and labor. Centrists, who believe that the truth is somewhere in the middle, are even less interested in the topic of work because they do not encounter it as a strong concern in the tensions between conservatives and liberals that they are trying to mediate.

The media reflect these attitudes. If someone not familiar with humanity were to watch television, they would assume that human life was about anything but work. With few exceptions, cultural production in literature, theater, music, and other venues is rarely focusing on work either. Not even the news reports are in the habit of reporting much about work: the business sections of the newspapers, for instance, do not tell us much about what is happening at work.

As a result, work is off almost everybody's radar screen. Work is treated as a nonissue at worst, or as a matter of special interests at best. When people hear the word *labor*, many tend to think of factory workers in blue overalls carrying old-fashioned lunch boxes. Others may think of immigrant workers who are frequently accused of taking away the jobs of Americans. Others still might think of low-wage workers at Walmart or in the fast-food industry. Except for some younger professionals whose work still earns them some satisfaction and prestige, it seems that fewer and fewer people today like to think about work or be asked the question "What do you do?" If in polite company the topics of politics and religion should not be mentioned, today this may be true to an even greater degree for the topic of work and labor, and talking about politics, religion, and labor together seems virtually impossible.

Nothing Matters More

At the same time, nothing matters more than work and labor. This might seem like an overstatement, but we are prepared to back it up. While we do not want to romanticize work (and neither do we want to deify or essentialize it), this book is an extended argument about why work matters in all areas of life and how to reclaim the value of work. Work is a central factor not just in economics and politics but also in culture, religion, and in our communities. We will come back to the limits of work soon.

Human life as we know it would not exist without work and labor. Producing and consuming food requires work, manufacturing shelter and clothing requires work, educating the next generations requires work, and even maintaining culture, communication, and relationships requires work. More than 99 percent of the world's population and most people who are reading this book have no choice but to work for a living. Even most of the less-than-1 percent who do not need to work for a living because of their affluence and wealth choose to work as well, and the ones who choose not to work could not exist without the work of the working majority.

Moreover, work shapes us deeply, all the way down. Work is likely the place where we experience power most intensely and in all of its shapes and forms, work is where domination and subordination is most palpably manifest in our lives, and work is where our subjectivity is formed to a large degree. Work is the place where others tell us what to do or where we have some power to tell others what to do, often with the assumption that this is the way the world works by default. Even in less top-down relationships at work, it is usually clear who is in charge and who is not. Questioning power at work is seen as mostly futile, unlike power in most other areas of life.

How we are shaped at work has implications for how we behave at home, in church, in community, in our families, and for how we think and believe. Men who experience dominance at work often embody it at home in relation to women and children. Many religious communities reflect how power is exercised at work, with people who have power at work having power in their communities. Those who sit on boards in corporations usually also sit on boards in church. And even if such leaders are absent, others fill in for them and perpetuate similar kinds of power structures. Finally, how power is exercised at work tends to influence in subtle ways how people perceive God; even for working people, God is often modeled after images that combine traits of the immediate boss and the mostly invisible CEO.

So, what is going on, why are work and labor so undervalued today? Are we merely dealing with forgetfulness, with unavoidable entropy, or perhaps with some more troublesome reality like a repression of facts and conspiracy? We do not believe that the troubles of work and labor are owed to natural causes—too many people assume steamrolling and power-blocking at work are normal and nothing can be done about it—but some of the answers might surprise you. To be sure, we do not ask this question out of sheer curiosity or sensationalism but because we are interested in learning what we can do as communities to turn the tide. The good news is that the tide may have already begun to turn and that there is support from budding social movements and even from a growing number of communities of faith that are waking up.

What we are trying to do in this book is to build on these awakenings and to take them to the next step. This is necessary, we believe, because awakenings without support and reflection will fizzle and fade quickly. For social movements this means that we need to sharpen our understanding of what energizes them and how this energy can be organized so that it can push against the system and impact it at its core. For faith communities this means that we need to reflect on what is at the roots of faith, which means radically rethinking images of God, community, and faith itself.[3] We are worried, from experience, that too many well-meaning people and even leaders and organizers are afraid (or perhaps merely too busy) to ask these questions.

Throughout history, work, working people, and even religions that care about work have shaped the world deeply, even though our histories have often been written from the perspective of those who made others do the work. Contrary to the way the stories are told, Caesar did not build the Roman Empire alone, and neither did the bishops and their theologians shape the fortunes of Christianity singlehandedly, just as little as they constructed the medieval cathedrals in Europe with their own hands. There is good reason to anticipate that the world of the future will once again be built by work, working people, and religions that care about work, no matter how much the power brokers of today would like to convince us otherwise.

There is no escape from work. Businesspeople and economists who neglect the fundamental contributions of work and workers, for instance by cutting salaries and benefits, have been creating growing problems that cannot be resolved long-term. Politicians who neglect the world of work and of workers are finding it difficult to build a strong democratic basis, resulting in the inordinate dependency of politics on corporations and big money that we are experiencing at present and that will keep haunting us for a long time to come. Faith leaders who neglect the realities of work and of workers are producing fantastic religious bubbles that will eventually burst just like economic bubbles keep bursting in recession after recession. Quite a few of these bubbles have burst already as religious enterprises crumble (Robert Schuller's famous Crystal Cathedral in Garden Grove, California, went bankrupt in 2010, for instance,) but more bubbles are in the making every day.

As we reclaim the importance of work, we are fighting pending disasters and we are reclaiming values that many of us hold in common, like the values of human productivity and creativity, the sharing of power, relationship, community, and democracy[4] (political, economic, as well as religious).

In all these efforts, we find ourselves in the company of many people throughout history, including the leaders of various religious traditions like the prophets of the Hebrew Bible and the prophet Muhammad. The apostle Paul may serve as an example. Against the dominant logic of the Roman Empire, Paul argued that a healthy community cannot act like a body where the head says to the feet "I have no need of you" and the eyes say to the hand "I have no need of you" (1 Cor. 12:21). Here and elsewhere Paul leaves no doubt that work matters. What if religion were not primarily about pious ideas but about work, community, solidarity, alternative power that flows from the bottom up rather than the top down, and a new way of life?

It should not be too hard for us to follow Paul's logic: a head cannot thrive without feet, and eyes need hands in order to make a difference. For people of faith, Paul adds an astonishing claim about God, who has arranged the body not from the top down but from the bottom up, so that "if one member suffers, all suffer together with it; if one member is honored, all rejoice together with it" (1 Cor. 12:26). It seems that perhaps no one has understood Paul better than the labor unions, when they claim that "an injury to one is an injury to all."

Work, Labor, and Transformation

There is a transformative quality of work and labor that has revolutionary implications. Not surprisingly, today this quality is not merely overlooked but repressed. This is why we need to go beyond merely reclaiming the value of work and labor. If we are correct that humanity as we know it would not exist without work and labor, does it not make sense to suspect that work and labor must have had a more important role in shaping and reshaping humanity than most of us realize?

If work and labor, as we are arguing in this book, shape us all the way to the core, they are not just a matter of economics—earning and spending money—but also a matter of politics, culture, religion, and even psychology. Spending the bulk of our waking hours at work influences who we are as individuals and communities, shapes the images of our cultures and faiths, and defines us in more ways than we can count.

In hunter and gatherer societies, work was fundamentally different from work in agrarian societies, and economics, politics, and religion adapted accordingly. Trade, power, and images of the divine become more centralized and more complex in agrarian societies. Work in feudal societies, where peasants had to carry the heaviest burdens yet have some self-determination because of social bonds and some communally owned land, was once again fundamentally different from work in capitalist societies, and economics, politics, culture, and religion shaped up accordingly. Once again, trade, power, and images of the divine shifted, enabling greater mobility on the one hand but also new arrangements of power where "winners take all."

Today, under the conditions of a capitalism that reaches into virtually every corner of the globe, people who work can no longer rely on traditional communal bonds. Since they also lack substantial wealth and savings, most have little more to sustain them than their labor power. In the United States increasing numbers of people, including members of the middle class and people with college degrees are only a few paychecks away from financial disaster. At the same time, the wealthy get wealthier, a process that has once again accelerated with the onset of the Great Recession in 2007 and its aftermath. These dynamics have implications not only for economics but also for politics and religion, which are linked in these disasters. Will economics, politics, and religion support these trends, as they often do, and further strengthen the power of the 1 percent by funneling money, power, and prestige to the top? Or will economics, politics, and religion work in support of the 99 percent?

The good news is that a growing number of alternatives exist today where work and labor already play a more positive role and where they are gaining new value and appreciation. One example of these developments is how some workers are starting their own enterprises and building worker-owned companies. There are plenty of examples, even in the United States, where we are now counting thousands of such companies. Many of these companies are still small, but there are also larger ones. In 2015, the top one hundred employee-owned companies in the United States employed 626,000 people.[5] The most well known is the Mondragon Corporation in Spain that employs over 70,000 people and has proven to be economically successful. Another example of work and labor gaining in value and power is when working people pull together, organizing, and developing new forms of communal power at their various places of work. In this book we will focus mostly on this latter topic, organizing and developing power.

What makes work and labor transformative or revolutionary today? The short answer is that work is what allows people to use their abilities (as well as their disabilities!) in productive fashion for the common good, which increases the welfare of the community and of the planet as a whole.[6] What is transformative here is not only in talking about the common good—capitalism also talks about the common good and claims that it is furthered when money and power are funneled to the top, assuming that if the wealthy are doing better everybody else is doing better by default. What is transformative about our view of work and labor is that we are putting the common good on wider and more robust foundations.

Shifting to a greater appreciation of the value of the work and the power of the working majority changes everything. This is true not only for economics but also politics, and ultimately even for religion. Consider the following points:

An economy that is based on valuing the work of everyone creates a climate where people matter and work cannot be as easily exploited. While many current debates are hung up on the problem of wealth and its distribution and redistribution, we want to shift the debate from distribution to production. Rather than talking about sharing wealth, we now can go to the roots of the problem and talk about how wealth is created in the first place, and who produces it. What does the working majority contribute to producing the common good and how is their work valued?[7] Why should a CEO have a salary that is hundreds of times that of an average worker, and why should a top investor make over twenty-thousand times as much money as that worker?[8] Not even capitalism has always sported such tremendous inequalities. In the 1965 CEOs had salaries that were merely twenty times larger than those of their workers.[9] Few other systems in history would have endorsed the inequalities that we see today. In the Roman Empire, the top 1 percent owned merely 16 percent of all wealth, compared to the top 1 percent owning 40 percent of all wealth in the United States today.[10] Why should economics equal inequality?

More than money is at stake, however, when it comes to the productive and transformative character of work. In addition to income, work also determines politics and the influence that people have in various contexts, including their own lives. If working people have some influence over their work, as they do in some places,[11] chances are that their voices will also carry some weight in their communities and that they will gain some influence in matters of politics. Such influence can be seen in benefits like paid sick leaves and vacation days, weekends off work, pension plans, and various protections against unfair and unsafe labor practices that were negotiated by the organized power of working people during the past one hundred years. Valuing working people who put their abilities to use for the common good means valuing alternative power, a kind of power that is not in the hands of the few but of the many. Is it possible to have true democracy any other way?

Religion, finally, changes as well when work is valued. No longer is religion about the ideas and values of the elites that are proclaimed to the people; religion, when it is tied to work, can link to matters of community, solidarity, alternative power, and new ways of life for everyone. From this perspective we can see many of the core traditions of religion in new light and reclaim them. In various traditions God is envisioned as a worker rather than as a monarch or a modern CEO. In some of the creation stories that are shared by Jews, Christians, and Muslims for instance, God is portrayed as a worker who produces Adam from the dust of the ground, rather than a manager who orders someone else to do the work. Judaism and Christianity also share traditions in which God plants a garden. Jesus in the Christian traditions was a construction worker who spent his life in solidarity with varieties of working people, refusing to move "up and out." If Jesus was fully human and fully divine, as many Christians believe, Godself became a construction worker in Jesus's life and ministry. If it is true that in many religious traditions work is not only a matter of subsistence but also a way of life and a matter of flourishing,[12] what happens to a religion that neglects work?

Another transformative aspect of work is that it has the potential to reshape our desires, which are those parts of our personal identities that we often take for granted. Despite the fact that capitalism constantly battles for our desires, at their core the desires of working people are different from the desires attributed to business leaders or to the leaders of religious communities. The deepest desire of working people is not the infinite maximization of profit, even though working people are not necessarily opposed to wealth; likewise, the deepest desire of the laity ("the people" in Greek) in religious communities is hardly the increase of membership rolls and budgets at all cost. The desire of working people as well as the laity relates more likely to the ability to do productive work that provides fair compensation and benefits and that provides for the welfare of families and communities.

Productive work that respects working people and their communities will also give more room to people's creativity. This creativity exists even under difficult working conditions, where workers often contribute significantly to improvements in the production of goods, ideas, and services despite not being treated with respect and fairness. There is a great deal of untapped potential in productive work. Part of this untapped potential is the transformation of desire and the production of alternative desire that is set free when work and labor are valued and respected.

Paying more attention to production and work and to how work binds us together does not mean that people should all be alike or that differences no longer matter. The opposite is the case: appreciating everyone's work—no matter how insignificant capitalism might want to make it appear—helps us take into account our differences in more positive fashion. Clearly, people have very different abilities and interests, and there is nothing wrong with pursuing them. Even people whom society considers disabled are now able to play a role, as they too would rather make contributions to the common good than depend on welfare from others. Moreover, people with disabilities might help us transform work and labor in ways that we cannot fully imagine yet.

When all work is valued and appreciated for the contributions it makes to human life and flourishing as well as to the common good, things change: everybody works, doing what they are good at and what they like to do, without constantly having to worry about being able to make ends meet. This attitude is summarized in a famous statement that predates Karl Marx, who popularized it: "From each according to their abilities, to each according to their need." Let us not forget that if virtually everybody works no one needs to be overworked while others are unemployed, and there is plenty of room for other activities outside of what might be considered work proper.

The Limits of Work and Labor

While work and labor are more important than many people realize, we should not forget about the dangers related to overestimating their value. The challenge we face is twofold: How do we fight the widespread devaluation of work and labor on the one hand and how do we avoid work and labor becoming the only things that matter in life? Expressed in the language of people of faith, *How do we make sure that work and labor do not become God?*

In some cases, the appreciation of work has been used in the exploitation and even in the destruction of work. During the German Third Reich for instance, one of the darkest chapters of human history, the motto posted at the entrance of several concentration camps was "*Arbeit macht frei*," "work liberates." The destruction of people through work remains a serious problem today, even if in most cases the destruction is not as visible as in the German concentration camps.

Paul Lafargue, Karl Marx's son-in-law, warned of this problem over a century ago. His essay titled "The Right to be Lazy" argues that the love for work has hurt workers and made them more exploitable. Lafargue talks about capitalism as a religion that commands working persons to "toil from early childhood to [their] dying day," suppressing any other aspirations for their family or themselves. The religion of capitalism, he notes, demands that those who are idle be excommunicated. Even taking time for prayer is frowned upon in this religion because it would be a waste of time; here, work becomes prayer.[13] Even Protestantism, Lafargue notes, has collaborated with the religion of capitalism by abandoning the feast days of the saints, which used to give people time off from work.[14]

In more recent times, feminists have reminded us again of the limits of work. According to Kathi Weeks, "the willingness to live for and through work renders subjects supremely functional for capitalist purposes."[15] When work is controlled by the dominant system, those who define themselves by it become defined by the system. Pointing out the limits of work in a capitalist society leads us to a new valuation of work. Feminists like Weeks remind us of the value of reproductive labor that is usually assigned to women, like childbearing and rearing and household work. Capitalism is more interested in productive labor because it feeds directly into the maximization of profits for corporations, thus neglecting reproductive labor. If productive labor is not valued sufficiently today, as we have argued, we need to remember that reproductive is valued even less.

Thinking about the limits of productive labor in a capitalist system leads us to rethink the value of reproductive labor, which also includes the so-called informal labor sector and casual labor. Much of this work is still done by women after coming home from work, like caring for children and managing the household. Women of the 99 percent share many of these experiences, no matter how enlightened their families and how supportive their husbands are.

Rosemarie recalls that as a new mother she was torn between returning to work picking up her project in the lab and staying home a few extra months to make sure our twin daughters got the best possible start and care that (supposedly) only a mother can give. She decided reluctantly to stay home with unpaid leave. And while she enjoyed being there for the children every day, she also knew that her absence in the lab was seen as a setback for the project. Her male colleagues never felt the same pressure when their children were home with their wives or at child care. For women on maternity leave, and increasingly for men on paternity leave, capitalist disregard for reproductive labor puts a lot of pressure on them to get back to work quickly. Staying at home with the kids is supposedly a selfish luxury.[16]

Women of racial and ethnic minorities are experiencing these pressures most severely. Womanist ethicist Joan Martin warns of the dangers of a "neo-work ethic" that is often used against black women, who are forced to bear the brunt of the burden of work.[17] Black and Latina women, for instance, frequently care for the children of others while making minimum wage, only to return home in order to care for their own children after hours. We strongly agree with Martin that our understanding of work and labor must be guided by working people who experience these pressures in their own bodies.[18]

The value of reproductive labor reminds us that the broader context of work is not production of things but the production of life itself. In the words of Weeks: "Life is part of work and work is part of life."[19] We might add that this could be the deeper meaning of the feminist mantra that the personal is the political; there is a political lesson in taking reproductive labor seriously. When work supports our lives, rather than consumes lives, the transformative capacities of work become clearer. Improvising on a saying of Jesus, we might argue that human beings are not created for work but work is created for human beings (Mark 2:27).

This means that reducing the time that people spend at work for their employers is one of the important struggles of our time.[20] The eight-hour workday is one of the milestones of modern labor history, which today is under attack again. Reversing history, people are expected to work more, including white-collar workers and salaried workers who deem themselves members of the middle class. Those who have vacation time are often afraid to use it, worried about repercussions from the top or about coworkers moving into their positions.

Though it has become the norm, there is no reason why people need to work eight hours. Three decades ago in Europe almost everyone assumed that workdays of seven or even six hours would be possible, and today some experiments with fewer hours at work with the same pay are still conducted.[21] Lafargue claims that three hours of work a day would be sufficient, and this number is not as unreasonable as it may sound at first.[22] Lafargue, an atheist, finds this work ethic modeled in Jesus's Sermon on the Mount, which he quotes: "Consider the lilies of the field, how they grow: they toil not, neither do they spin: and yet I say unto you that even Solomon in all his glory was not arrayed like one of these."[23] Lafargue adds that God rested after six days of work, assuming that this means that God rests for all eternity. While we do not agree with this latter notion, the matter of rest and taking time for doing things other than work is hard to dispute.

By limiting work hours two things are accomplished: The first is that people rather than the corporations reap the benefits from the employment of technology and machines in the workplace. The second is that more people will be able to join the labor force and be productive, thus reducing the despair of long-term unemployment and the need to prevent people with disabilities and others from working.

The other side of limiting work time is the need to increase the compensation for waged workers who work overtime. Recently the United States Department of Labor has begun making sure that workers who do work overtime are fairly compensated and not misclassified "managers" by their employers in order to circumvent extra pay for extra hours. For many salaried white collar and exempt workers toiling long and hard hours is the badge of being a good employee, one who exceeds the norm in order to make the company great. Rosemarie recalls the culture of work at a small start-up biotech company where she worked for a few years, where the pressure was always on to work late hours for the benefit of the project. Employees who came in early to beat traffic and left early to take care of the kids were seen as slackers, accused of not caring about the progress of the company and the project as a whole.

Valuing work and acknowledging the limits of work, thus, need to go hand in hand. In other words, work becomes more valuable when limits are established and honored.

Freedom Is Not Free and Organizing Is Not Optional

Americans are proud of their freedom and many would consider the United States the country on earth that enjoys the most freedoms. Most would also agree that freedom does not come easy and needs to be fought for. Unfortunately, the freedom that is most commonly fought for these days, not only on the battlefields of war but also in the courtrooms and in legislative sessions, is the freedom of corporations from limitations and regulations. The freedom of working people, on the other hand, is rarely even considered an issue. The shocking truth is that this freedom is more restricted in the United States than in virtually any other developed country. This is no accident, as we will see.

While corporations in the United States enjoy unheard of freedoms and continue to push against any and all regulations, workers enjoy surprisingly little freedom. To put it bluntly: capital is free to do things that working people are not. Unlike capital, working people are not yet free to affiliate and to organize. Unlike capital, working people are not free to move freely across borders and find work elsewhere, as established by various free trade agreements. The minority of working people today who enjoy the right to organize—as well as those who feel that they may not need to organize— should never forget that no one is free until all are free, as Martin Luther King Jr., used to say.

The most blatant restrictions of the freedom of working people in the United States are found where they are trying to organize. We are not aware of any other country that imposes such heavy restrictions on the freedom of working people to organize. The current legal situation makes it difficult for working people even to put their heads together and to associate with each other. Making their voices heard as a community is mostly prohibited. Forming a union, which allows working people to affiliate and to speak out as a group, is so difficult that only half a million workers succeed each year, out of twenty-five to sixty million workers who would like to do so.[24] Many jobs are excluded from forming unions altogether, including workers who have managerial duties, another oddity of US law. Even forming organizations that are merely associations without the privileges of a union is difficult, as the experiences of Walmart workers have shown.[25] An additional impediment to the freedom of working people has to do with extremely powerful efforts by employers to subvert unionization (also called union busting) by hiring experts and granting them virtually unlimited access to their workforce.

Antiunion laws restricting the freedom of working people to organize are the result of employers who are organized and their efforts to control what is happening at work. None of these laws fell from heaven and none of them were part of the Constitution of the United States, which guarantees freedom of association. In fact, these restrictions of freedom are so severe that they amount to a clear violation of the Human Rights Charter of the United Nations, which states that workers must have the right to form and join trade unions.[26]

In this climate, it comes as a surprise and it is not widely known that most of the major religious communities in the United States agree with working people's right to form unions and to bargain collectively. These communities include the Roman Catholic Church, the United Methodist

Church (UMC), the Christian Methodist Episcopal Church (CME), the Episcopal Church, the American Baptist Churches, USA, the Unitarian Universalists, the Evangelical Lutheran Church of America (ELCA), the Presbyterian Church (USA), the United Church of Christ, the Christian Church (Disciples of Christ), the Church of the Brethren. [27] In 2005, the Union for Reform Judaism at its 68th General Assembly explicitly passed its support for the right to organize and bargain collectively. [28]

The good news is that none of the restrictions have completely managed to prevent people from sticking their heads together, affiliating with each other, supporting each other, and speaking out. Humans are social beings after all, and we cannot be divided indefinitely. This is where the task of organizing starts, but we cannot stop there.

More is at stake, however, than merely collective bargaining. The challenge is to reclaim work and its transformative potential. This will take some collective effort. Contrary to what Hollywood has led us to believe, no superhero and no strong individual leader will appear and fix things according to our wishes. History shows that nothing will change without working people collaborating and organizing. Without organized working people, today there would be no eight-hour workdays, no weekends off work, no sick leaves or parental leaves, and child labor might still be around in the United States. The list continues. The 99 percent will only be successful if a critical mass manages to pool its power. This flies directly in the face of our American belief in the abilities and powers of strong individuals to take things into their own hands. This is the work ethic of the white American patriarchal "self-made man."

The work ethic of the self-made man is the ethic of the elites, which is fundamentally different from a work ethic that benefits the 99 percent of us who need to work for a living. According to this ethic, which is the ethic of individualism, people are able to pull themselves up "by their own bootstraps." The elites want everyone to believe that this is precisely what happened in their cases, that they have earned their wealth and their power by working longer and harder than all others. This belief supports the growing gap between the 99 percent and the 1 percent. According to this point of view, the individual trumps the community.

The truth, of course, is that these elites are not the autonomous individuals they claim to be. There are no self-made individuals anywhere in this world, as success is always produced in relation to others and with their help, starting with parents who raise their children and confer their privileges to them, continuing with teachers and the networks that people build in school and college, including fraternities, sororities, religious communities, and many other social organizations. Additionally, the success of businesses and corporations is built in relation to the people who work for them, as profit is achieved through the difference between what workers are paid and the value of that which they produce. Put all of this together and it should be clear that the ethic of individualism is a cover-up for how capitalism actually functions.

Elites can get away with the myth of individualism because they have greater resources and more power to promote their point of view than most working people. Working people, on the other hand, only harm themselves and their communities when they think of themselves as individuals and try to act like it. No matter how powerful and valued people who work for a living may feel, they will never be on equal footing with their employers, no matter whether they are Walmart workers or tenured university professors. This matters especially when there are conflicts of interest, of which there are many in the world of unregulated capitalism where the rule is "winner takes all" and where stockholder interest trumps worker interest.

Working people, from Walmart workers to university professors, will only make a difference when they pull together and learn to organize, and they will only understand the need to organize when they realize that individualism is a pernicious myth, designed to keep them powerless. In these efforts they might learn some lessons from the elites who, despite their endorsements of individualism, tend to be much more organized and connected than most people realize. The elites live according to old rule that it does not matter how much one knows but whom one knows. Social organizations including elite country clubs, sororities and fraternities at universities, and even religious communities are heavily used for maintaining the power of the 1 percent. Other organizations that are more directly focused on action include the American Legislative Exchange Council (ALEC) and various think tanks.

Ancient Wisdom at Work

In this book we seek to bring some ancient wisdom to bear on the matter of organizing, helping work reclaim its transformative impact. The Abrahamic religions of Judaism, Christianity, and Islam[29] will guide us, because of their deep involvement in matters of work and labor that include fresh perspectives on the divine. While we are limiting ourselves in this volume to three religions, we encourage and invite engagement of other religious traditions as well. Engagements with Engaged Buddhism, for instance, have proven fruitful in some settings.

These ancient insights not only show how old the need for organizing is for working people, they also shed some light on how organizing has helped humanity flourish throughout the ages. Moreover, these ancient insights can inform and inspire modern ones, helping us realize that the universe works differently from what we are usually taught in the media, schools, social clubs, and religious communities.

A parable that Jesus tells in the Gospel of Matthew may serve as an example of how ancient wisdom is still powerful. This parable is about a service worker who is unwilling to forgive another worker (Matt. 18:23–35). In this unusual story a boss forgives a worker an enormous amount of debt. This usually does not happen in the world of working people. In this case, however, the worker whose debt has been forgiven now has a choice, which he did not have before. When a coworker approaches him about the forgiveness of a much smaller debt, this worker is now free either to forgive or collect the debt. In the parable, the worker chooses to collect the debt from his coworker rather than to forgive it. Since the fellow worker cannot pay, he has him thrown in prison, thus following the logic of individualism that is the logic of the powerful.

There is, however, another logic here that we would call the logic of organizing, which is the logic of those who are often considered powerless. Following this logic, the better choice would have been to forgive the debt of the fellow worker. The reasoning is simple but only works when we see through the false promises of individualism. Not forgiving the fellow worker's debt results in every worker having to fight on his or her own. The worker who collected the small debt now has a small amount of money but he loses something much more valuable, namely solidarity. Forgiving the debt would create solidarity among workers and would establish a relationship and a community where people support each other and help each other out when they are in need.

This is what we mean by organizing: forging bonds among people that support the common good and building the power able to sustain it. To return to the parable: If the boss were to change his mind at some point in the future and start indebting workers again, the solidarity of the workers is the only thing that counts, as money is quickly spent and gone.

In this parable the worker whose debt is forgiven is the only one who does not seem to realize what is going on. The other workers understand what is happening and protest his actions. It seems to us that Jesus tells this parable in order to help people grasp the basic principles of organizing that some understand better than others. Working people who experience powerlessness may have a head start, but all of us need to keep learning.

The good news embodied in this parable is that we do not need to make a case for organizing by moralizing. It is not necessary to tell people what they should or should not do based on someone else's great ideas. According to this parable, we can realize the need for organizing and how to organize by opening our eyes and by observing what is actually going on and then act in ways that are in our best interests and actually make sense. This is an advantage that organizers can employ at all times, and this is one of the main lessons for religious leaders who are prone to moralizing. Moralizing hardly leads to transformation, and organizing is not about moralizing!

Organizing is something that people who have to work for a living—the 99 percent, i.e., virtually everyone who reads this book—can learn and understand because it is life-giving to them. This insight is the key to the transformative potential of work. Bosses (and bankers), on the other hand, have a more difficult time learning, yet they too can join the transformation if they give up the logic of the powerful.

Preachers who think from the perspective of the powerful face similar difficulties. Their attempts to moralize about Jesus's parable of the unforgiving servant falter in most cases. Here is how they usually argue: someone has forgiven you a great debt, now you are morally required to forgive as well, even if it is not in your best interest. Such moralizing did not work with the government bailouts during the Great Recession—the financial institutions whose debt was forgiven did not forgive others—and it is not likely to work in the world of business today.

The logic of the powerless, on the other hand, was more successful. When the 99 percent began to organize, debt was actually forgiven. One of the most successful campaigns during the height of the Occupy Wall Street movement was buying up student debt and then forgiving it.[30]

Unfortunately, the logic of the powerful and of individualism is still widespread and can even be found in labor unions and churches. Jesus' parable of the unforgiving servant describes a real problem. Many workers join unions because they think it helps them gain personal advantages, and some quit the union when they think they got what they wanted. This is not surprising because the power of solidarity and organizing is rarely taught anywhere, beginning with our schools all the way to our religious communities. The only way to overcome this false consciousness is to learn how to think again from the perspective of work and working people. If the workers in Jesus's day were able to understand, why should working people today not also be able to learn?

And, as Jesus's parable also seems to indicate, even bosses can sometimes get it. If God is someone who forgives debt— one of the greatest tools for maintaining top-down power— we need to change our view of the world. One of the most interesting contemporary insights into the person of Jesus is that he was an organizer, not merely a radical preacher. This is what made him dangerous to the Romans who punished other radical preachers but did not kill them.[31]

What if the world is not about maintaining top-down power but with a bottom-up sort of power, creating solidarity that ties working people together, and leading to stronger communities where productivity and creativity are valued rather than dominance, including sharing power, forming relationships, and democracy? We will come back to that idea when we talk about the power of deep solidarity.

CHAPTER 2

Work under Attack: Dire Consequences

No Natural Catastrophe

Why are work and labor undervalued today? We left this question somewhat open earlier, noting that we are not dealing with a natural catastrophe. Is that not, however, what many people assume, namely that the current troubles for work and labor are natural and that not much can be done about them? We will argue that work is not losing is value and its power because of some law of nature but because it is under attack

Things were not always as they are now. Long hours at work,[1] for instance, developed over time and the time people spend at work ebbs and flows in different periods. From the sixteenth through the nineteenth centuries, people were forced to work longer and longer hours. The struggle for the maximization of private profit, which defines capitalism, picked up in those years and put increasing pressures on the working majority. Today, this history continues and the battles are fought in new ways. Well paying jobs in manufacturing (many of them union organized) are moved overseas where labor is cheaper, for instance, guaranteeing new gains in the struggle for profit. What is often termed "the race to the bottom" is picking up speed.

Increasingly, jobs are moved to the South of the United States, since wages are lower there than in the North, and workers are less likely to have power that comes through union and community organizing. The cost of labor in these states is becoming more competitive with global wages since wages have virtually stagnated since the seventies while productivity has steadily increased. As a result, some work is returning again to the United States from overseas. Unfortunately, in many cases this work no longer supports a family. In Dallas, Texas, as mentioned earlier, child poverty is at 38 percent, the highest in the nation for cities over one million residents.[2] And most of the parents of these children are working, since the unemployment rate hovers around 3.5 percent, according to the U.S. Bureau of Labor Statistics![3]

Things were not always this bad. In more recent history, beginning with the late nineteenth century, there was a time when work and working people enjoyed some appreciation and when the minimum wage was designed to sustain a family at a very basic level. There was a time when the eight-hour workday was the standard and when weekends were respected. Of course, this was not due to natural developments either. Work and working people were appreciated because many of the communities, including religious communities, understood that workers matter to their well-being. Moreover, working people enjoyed some respect because they were organized, which gave them power and standing in the community.

During the past decades, however, things have changed dramatically. Work and working people only became more valuable as their productivity increased: between 1973 and 2014 productivity at work has grown 72.2 percent. Based on this information, it would be reasonable to expect that this increase in value would have led to an increase of compensation and benefits. What actually happened, however, was the opposite. As work and working people became more valuable to their employers, their hourly compensation increased a mere 9.2 percent, which does not even account for inflation. In other words, while the value of labor increased exponentially, compensation for labor decreased in comparison.[4]

Employers might point out in response that what has come under pressure in neoliberal capitalism[5] is not just work but also their profit margins. Competition has indeed gotten fiercer nationally and internationally. The rest of us might respond, in turn, that these pressures have been unfairly distributed, as profit margins have continued to increase at a substantial pace while worker compensation has not. Moreover, the trickle down of wealth from top to bottom— the justification economists use to find value in growing inequality—has never happened. Today, when the inequality between employers and employees is at a peak, we are still not able to observe any meaningful or measurable transfer from top to bottom. On the contrary, all we are seeing is growing income inequality with the gains of productivity growth going to the top, to the major owners of capital. Politicians of both parties are now in agreement on this.[6]

One of the key reasons why profits keep increasing at the top has to do with pressure being put on work and labor. In order to do this, the value of work and labor needs to be played down. The paradox is that even though labor today is more valuable than ever, the general opinion holds that labor is not worth much and that many workers lack skill and zeal. This makes it easy to increase the pressure on labor and to skew the delicate relationship between employers and employed even further. The problem is that profits are valued over people.

This unequal relationship between employers and employed is at the heart of capitalism and its quest for the maximization of private profit. Today more than ever, most economists consider the relation a zero-sum game: profit for employers and stockholders can only grow when workers earn less. Consequently, whenever the position of working people grows stronger, this is seen as bad news for business. No wonder the pressures on work and working people keep increasing. This is true not only for low-income workers, whose precarious situation is often discussed today, but for almost anyone else who belongs to the 99 percent. Even professionals, such as doctors and academics, are experiencing pressure, to the point that these groups are also forming unions in order to assert some collective influence over their work and over the corporations managing it.[7]

This reality is missed whenever inequalities of the current situation are blamed on personal greed, particularly the greed of employers. While blaming greed may be the easiest way to make a point, we are not joining that chorus here. While we do not endorse greed, our point is that the problem is much greater and much more serious and that focusing on individuals and their immoral behavior can distract from the bigger issues. Too often, working people challenge their employers only when they perceive them to be greedy, yet they support them when they think they are merely acting according to economic necessity. This is true especially for working people who are religious.[8]

The Law

The unequal relationship between employers and employees is manifested in policy decisions that substantially reduce the bargaining power of working people and increase the powers of corporations. Among these are the so-called "Right to Work" laws and employment-at-will laws. In the twenty-four Right to Work states in the United States it is unlawful to make union membership a condition of employment. If people are employed at a factory that is unionized, they can refuse to join the union, but they will still benefit from the contract that the union has negotiated for all workers at the plant. Many workers take the benefits negotiated without supporting the structure that made it possible, often resulting in the financial demise of unions. Employment-at-will means that an employer does not need good cause to fire workers, further shifting power to the employer. Most states recognize employment-at-will unless employment contracts specify a different process, which union contracts regularly spell out in detail to protect the worker.

Other laws also back up the power differentials between employers and workers, enabling the skewed valuation of production. The National Labor Relations Act (NLRA), passed in 1935 and later modified in 1947 with the Taft-Hartley amendment, secures the right of workers to organize and bargain collectively. However, roughly one in four workers are left out of these protections, denying their constitutional right of freedom of association. The workers left out, who are able to organize in most other countries, include supervisors and managers, small business employees, independent contractors, agricultural workers, domestic workers, and a significant number of public employees. In today's economy, the numbers of these workers continue to grow.[9]

It is interesting to note that while there are plenty of laws that limit the formation of unions and bargaining agreements, there are no legal incentives for employers to recognize unions or to reach bargaining agreements.

At the same time as policy decisions continue to erode support for workers and their organizations, support for corporations is growing. One example is the US Supreme Court's dramatic expansion of personhood rights to corporations. Among other things, this makes it easier for corporations to exert power by influencing democratic elections through spending money in candidate elections.[10] Other consequences of this development include the right of corporations to determine matters that touch on the personal lives of their employees. Some corporations, for instance, have won the legal right to refuse birth control coverage in employee health-care plans based on religious grounds.[11] However one feels about the argument that corporations "are organizations of people, and the people should not be deprived of their constitutional rights when they act collectively,"[12] it is interesting that the same personhood rights are not given to unions, which are organizations of people as well.

Finally, while not a law *per se*, it has become the generally accepted dogma for corporations that their primary responsibility is to their stockholders rather than to their workers. The legal precedent is a ruling of the Michigan Supreme Court in 1919 against Henry Ford, stating, "A business corporation is organized and carried on primarily for the profit of the stockholders."[13] Economist Milton Friedman, one of the fathers of neoliberal economics, also put his weight behind this position. One of his articles, titled "The Social Responsibility of Business Is to Increase its Profits," published in the *Wall Street Journal* in 1970, has also been cited in support of the interest of stockholders over and against workers.[14] This means that for corporations the concerns of workers and their treatment as employees must be considered secondary.

In sum, US law is increasingly supporting the position of the stockholders, in particular those who are holding the large chunks or the majority of stock who are ultimately the owners of the corporations. These are also called job creators—corporations need workers, after all—yet they are creating the kinds of jobs that lead to an ever-increasing wage and power gap between employers and workers.

These shifts in the law often go unrecognized, even by those who are most affected by them. Informal surveys that have been done in Dallas by several community groups, for instance, found concerns about many issues, including predatory lending and lack of support for education and health care. Much less frequently expressed were concerns for jobs, fair wages, and benefits, and the overall role that the concerns of working people play both in the economy and in the political process.

The problem with the law as it stands is that it limits not only the power of working people, it also limits the value placed on the work that they do. If the production of workers were valued and fairly compensated according to the contributions they make to the economy, things would be very different. Since these matters go unrecognized, however, the debate shifts from the value of production to the distribution of resources. While many well-meaning people, including religious communities, argue for a more equal distribution of resources, these debates overlook the fundamental reasons why resources are not distributed justly and why even redistribution would not make a difference for very long when production is not valued accordingly.

Unfortunately, most of the media are of little help when it comes to creating public awareness for the current legal situation that translates into growing attacks on work. Given the epidemic proportions of the problems of wage theft and wage depression, what little reporting is going on about these problems is usually "balanced" with statements by management that these problems are not as bad as they seem. Many times we have seen news reports presenting testimonies by workers who share stories of being hurt on the job, of not being able to make ends meet, and of being prevented from working full-time even though there is plenty of work, conclude with statements from corporate spokespersons who offer no explanations but assure the public with authoritative demeanor that everything is fine.

Wage Theft as Symptom

Wage theft is the most obvious example of work under attack. It happens to millions of workers, especially the ones employed in the construction and service industries. Wage theft takes many forms, including withholding tips, forcing workers to work "off the clock," paying less than minimum wage, taking illegal deductions out of paychecks, and withholding payment after termination or work completed. Wage theft can help us get a first glimpse of how work is under attack. It is so clearly and blatantly wrong that no one will defend it openly. Because of the moral nature of the problem, creating an awareness of wage theft works almost anywhere, including more conservative faith communities.

A possible problem with discussing wage theft (similar to blaming greed) is that systemic problems are covered up and that some people can use their righteous outrage over wage theft (or greed) as an excuse not to have to deal with the deeper problems of neoliberal capitalism. For this reason, we need to keep in mind the connection between wage theft and wage depression from the outset. Wage theft can teach us about wage depression, which is a phenomenon that affects virtually everyone who is a member of the 99 percent. This is especially true for those two-thirds of Americans who belong to the so-called working class majority; it is also true, however, for the middle class who also belong to what we are calling the working majority. Even middle class jobs are under pressure, many of them no longer providing the benefits and securities that once existed.

Many people are surprised when they find out that wage theft is a rampant problem in twenty-first century America. Yet day after day millions of dollars are withheld and thus stolen from workers. Agriculture, poultry processing, janitorial services, restaurant work, garment manufacturing, long-term care, home health care, and retail are the industries with the most reported cases of wage theft. Wage theft occurs predominantly at nonunionized workplaces and in those industries that are excluded from the labor law.

The term *wage theft* has been coined by Kim Bobo, the founder of Interfaith Worker Justice. Bobo was one of the first to publicize the rampant stealing by employers of what workers had worked hard to earn and her book on the topic contains a wealth of information.[15] The wage-theft epidemic is not a natural phenomenon. One of its triggers has been the weakening of the labor movement. A unionized workforce has recourse through grievance procedures, collective action, and when necessary even strikes. However, reclaiming what was wrongfully taken by an employer is no simple task for the lone worker.

Just how great is this problem? A 2014 report by the Economic Policy Institute compares the dollars lost through crimes like burglary and robbery in 2012 to those lost through wage theft. The total value of the property taken in all reported robberies in the nation was slightly over $340 million. In comparison, approximately $933 million were recovered for the victims of wage theft. In other words, almost three times as much money was recovered and returned to workers in wage-theft cases than was stolen through robberies.[16] Yet not even these dramatic figures present the full amount of the problem, as the amount of wages recovered is much smaller than the amount actually stolen since most workers do not report wage theft and not everything is recovered.

With the founding of worker centers across the nation, many of them supported by Interfaith Worker Justice,[17] workers now have venues to get help when wage theft occurs, for instance through filing Department of Labor complaints and even lawsuits. Worker centers also help workers make their voices heard and get public attention. In Dallas, for instance, a branch of the Workers Defense Project based in Austin has been fighting various construction companies for back payment of stolen wages through direct action like large rallies with community and faith groups in front of construction sites or at company headquarters. Like other worker centers, the Workers Defense Project also trains workers and empowers them to negotiate with developers and elected officials.

Other organizations address wage theft as well. Our Jobs with Justice coalition in North Texas, for instance, has supported various actions of the Workers Defense Project when construction companies failed to pay workers. Actions like press conferences, collecting signatures on petitions supporting the workers' demands to receive the pay owed to them, sending letters to construction company management, and inviting workers who have been robbed on the job to share their stories at hearings, have helped to make the larger community aware of the criminal behavior of local construction companies. In Dallas and Austin, over $1 million in back wages have been reclaimed for over one thousand workers since its inception in 2002.[18]

In Texas, as in many other states around the country, the majority of these workers are undocumented and therefore an easy target for wage theft and other violations. As long as our immigration system has no legal path to long-term work permits and citizenship, unscrupulous employers will be able to take advantage of undocumented workers. Their fear of removal and separation from their families will keep them from speaking out and blowing the whistle.

Another problem with responding to wage theft is that it sometimes fails to go beyond the immediate situation to efforts to organize more broadly. Workers who are wronged may feel that things are back to normal when they have received their back pay. Many religious communities are open to hearing the stories of violated workers and respond with support but never venture very far beyond concrete examples of wage theft, to how to fix this particular problem. Attending rallies, sending letters, signing petitions, volunteering, and donating money are important but not sufficient responses.

While exposing and discussing wage theft and acting on it is a good start, we need to keep in mind the broader context in which workers are exploited. Wage theft is but the most blatant example of the devaluing of work and working people that is manifest in wage *depression,* which affects almost all of us. While most people agree that stealing wages is morally wrong, fewer engage the depression of wages because the problem is less obviously a moral issue. Too often, people are taking the widely promoted standpoints of the corporations, assuming that wage depression is necessary and even natural, without seeing possible links between wage theft and wage depression. We still need to bridge the gap between understanding moral wrongs committed by individual corporations and the systemic wrongs that keep working people from getting off the ground even when no laws are broken.

The wage-theft campaign has served as a wake-up call and helped mobilize faith communities as well as funders. Partnering with this campaign, the next step is to harness the success of the wage-theft campaigns with religious communities and the broader public constructively.

Wage Depression: The Next Step

Unlike wage theft, wage depression often takes place without violating the law. Like wage theft, wage depression is not a natural phenomenon. The term refers to widespread efforts to push down compensation for working people.

This happens at many levels of the economy. Many of the jobs that were lost in the Great Recession of recent memory never returned; what returned were jobs that carried the same responsibility but offered lower salaries, benefits, and less job security. At many universities, for instance, tenured professors are being replaced by adjunct professors, whose teaching load is higher but who earn merely a fraction and are only employed semester to semester, without any kind of job security or benefits. Computer programmers find their jobs outsourced to workers overseas whose salaries are significantly lower and who receive no benefits. And even when these programmers do not lose their jobs, outsourcing puts downward pressure on their wages. Many other well-paying jobs are undergoing similar pressures: there is now a two-tiered wage system in most auto manufacturing plants. As a radical cost-cutting measure to save the auto industry from its near collapse during the Great Recession, contracts were negotiated which created lower paying jobs for newly hired workers. These jobs also often came with second-class health and retirement benefits (or none at all) and were thought to be temporary. This practice is putting a great strain on solidarity between young and old workers and undermines the equalizing idea of equal pay for equal work. While the United Auto Workers and other unions are working to limit the use of two-tiered worker systems now that the automakers are profitable again, this practice continues to spread in industries such as retail, health, and airline, as well as in the public sector.

While there are many examples of wage depression, the best place to observe the phenomenon is at the bottom rungs of the economy. "As goes Walmart so goes the economy." This is a statement heard often in the context of the hardships faced by Walmart workers. It refers to the largest private employer of the world that is making enormous profits by pushing down wages, cutting or eliminating benefits, and preventing workers from full-time employment, thus forming an on-demand workforce with nontransparent scheduling. This model for treating workers is spreading into all other areas of work, not only blue collar but also white collar, including the middle class. These developments are linked to a growing loss of respect for work and for working people who are considered irresponsible, lazy, and undeserving, and they are linked to laws and policies that benefit corporations.

Walmart is ranked at the very top of global Fortune 500 companies according to its own website.[19] The company has 2.2 million employees and made $16.4 billion in profits in 2014. The combined wealth (in assets, capital, stock, and securities) of the six heirs of Sam Walton, the founder of the company, who hold more than 50 percent of the shares of the company, is greater than that of 42 percent of all Americans.

This means that six people own more than 49 million American families put together. Walmart's tremendous bargaining power derives from a combination of two facts: Walmart's enormous size and the concentration of wealth at the top of the company. Walmart not only determines the standards of the industry, it also serves as role model for corporations in other sectors.

While Walmart is thus one of the most successful companies of all time, its workers do not fare as well. According to a report, the average Walmart Associate makes just $8.81 per hour. Many workers get to only work thirty-four hours a week—Walmart's definition of full-time—which results in annual earnings of $15,500 per year.[20] Even people who get to work full-time at Walmart still live below the poverty line. Moreover, Walmart's wages help drive down wages across the retail spectrum and across the nation.[21]

There are other consequences of wage depression Walmart-style. Walmart's rock bottom wages may be costing average taxpayers between $900,000 and $1,750,000 per store while boosting profits for the corporation, according to a 2013 report by the Democratic staff of the United States House Committee on Education and the Workforce.[22] When workers are denied full-time work and for this reason are not eligible for health care and other benefits, they are unable to afford basic necessities and care. As a result, taxpayers are forced to pick up the difference because Walmart workers have no choice but to use emergency room care at public county hospitals and many must apply for public food assistance in order to feed their children.

Shortly before Thanksgiving in 2013 news broke that an Ohio Walmart store was asking associates to donate canned goods for their Walmart colleagues who were struggling to make ends meet.[23] It is actions like these that have given the public some insight into the plight of many Walmart workers.

Since the topic of our book is religion and labor, we need to keep in mind the religious overtones of the Walmart ethos. Over time Walmart has become the major distributor of mostly conservative Christian merchandise and books, putting out of business many independent Christian retail stores.[24] The use of religious principles in the company's ethos such as "servant leadership" (as a way of "furthering" career goals "through other people") and remaking shopping as "selfless service to family" have further helped to push Walmart to the top of the economy.[25] If religion and people of faith want to be part of the solution, we need to understand how religion has become part of the problem as well.

Another high-profile example for wage depression is the T-Mobile Corporation. There is a huge difference between how T-Mobile (Deutsche Telekom) workers are treated in Germany, where the corporation originated (30 percent of the shares of the corporation are still owned by the German government) and how T-Mobile workers are treated in the United States. The discrepancies between the workers in the two countries are stunning, far exceeding wage depression but contributing to it. In addition to lower wages, one of the key concerns of workers in the United States is job security, as they can be laid off at any time, unlike in Germany. While workers in Germany are unionized, the American arm of T-Mobile is fighting any efforts of their workers to unionize.[26] And while in Germany union representatives sit on the boards of the corporations, in the United States workers have virtually no input when it comes to the leadership of their corporation.

Joerg recalls a press conference in the Dallas-Fort Worth area where T-Mobile workers from Germany and the United States discussed the differences in working conditions, from the lack of rest breaks in the United States to the fact that German workers get two or three times more vacation than American workers. On this occasion, the German workers were accompanied not only by their union representatives but also by a member of the German Parliament. By contrast, not even local American politicians joined the American workers at the press conference, and Texas media ignored the event, so that the public never learned about the issues. Similar labor practices are used in a race to the bottom globally. German workers are put under pressure by outsourcing jobs to the United States, where labor is weaker, wages are lower, and benefits fewer. Workers from the north of the United States, where labor is still stronger, are put under pressure by sending jobs to the southern states, where the labor movement and labor laws are weaker. In response, the AFL-CIO in the United States has committed itself to a "Southern Strategy" at its national meeting in 2013, with an emphasis on organizing workers in the South. This strategy also includes investing in labor and community coalitions to initiate strategic campaigns on local levels that highlight discrepancies between public money investments and tax breaks and that help determine who will benefit from many of these projects. The American South is emerging as a battleground, since it is affected the most by this race to the bottom. Attention to religion is also a part of this Southern Strategy, since the majority of working people in the South are religious.

These examples of wage depression point us back to challenges to work everywhere. Wage depression affects not just low-wage workers. The pressures found at Walmart are also found in white-collar work. The Amazon corporation is a case in point, as it has made news for pushing its workers to new extremes. The goal is to increase productivity and to get more work done with less money. Along the way, everyone is continuously monitored and evaluated. Those who work for the company are encouraged to participate in this process, evaluating their coworkers and submitting reviews to their superiors.[27]

Reports about exciting new programs that grant new benefits and freedoms to employees at some of the nation's most profitable and forward-looking corporations like Netflix seem to counter these trends. Nevertheless, they have to be seen in the overall context. The widely-broadcasted benefits of these corporations like paid family leaves of several months, flexible work hours, etc., are only available to a very small number of employees—those who are considered "talent."[28] For all others, including those managers who are not in the top-ranked departments, the climate is very different and is more likely to resemble working conditions at Walmart and Amazon.

As responses to wage theft have been successful, millions of dollars of back wages have been recovered. Responses to wage depression have also had some success, but pushback has been much more pronounced. With most big businesses, this particular fight strikes a nerve.

Walmart may well be one of the most aggressive antiunion companies on the planet.[29] While Walmart claims to be protecting its associates by opposing unions, it is unclear why a company that does not seem to offer any special consideration for its employees would be so motivated to fight even the smallest effort of its workers to affiliate.

In 2012, North Texas Jobs with Justice made it a priority to support the local "Making Change at Walmart" campaign. Working closely with workers who organized as a nonunion association called Organization United for Respect at Walmart (OUR Walmart), we started calling on our members and allies to stand in solidarity with Walmart workers and to attend their rallies and Black Friday actions.

Immediately following the first rallies, Walmart filed complaints with the National Labor Relations Board, claiming that the United Food and Commercial Workers Union (UFCW) that supported OUR Walmart was intentionally seeking "to create an environment that could directly and adversely impact our [Walmart's] customers and associates."[30] From the very beginning, Walmart was determined to silence local workers and the community.

Our Jobs with Justice Chapter decided to see how much support there was for the demands of OUR Walmart from the community and from Walmart customers. We started collecting signatures for a petition that addressed the basic grievances of workers at Walmart, including respect on the job, transparent scheduling, full-time work, and better benefits and higher wages. To our surprise, it took almost no effort to get signatures for our petition. We had no difficulty explaining the concerns of Walmart workers to the majority of the public. Many had direct experience with working at Walmart or knew from a family member or friend what it was like being a Walmart associate, and they were happy to sign the petition.

The only person more surprised than us about this outcome was the Walmart store manager, to whom we presented the signed petitions. He could not believe that we were able to fill several pages of signatures in just a short period in his parking lot. The awareness of the success of this action and the strong public support led to pushback. Not long afterwards, Walmart filed an injunction against North Texas Jobs with Justice and its founder Gene Lantz, OUR Walmart, and the UFCW, barring us from entering Walmart parking lots and properties unless we were shopping there.

Walmart keeps disputing that any of these efforts have any impact on decisions at the top level. The business community and even the media support this position. When Walmart raised its lowest wages to $9 in early 2015 and promised a raise to $10 by February 2016, most commentators put down the organizing efforts of Walmart workers and the community and claimed Walmart was merely adjusting to the demands of the market. According to Ann C. Hodges, a labor relations expert at the University of Richmond quoted in *The New York Times*, "We're finally going to see a wage creep, and Walmart is trying to get out in front. They're thinking: We're probably going to do this anyway."[31]

However, how can anyone rule out that organizing made a difference in this case? Why should Walmart all of a sudden jump the gun on the issue of wage increases? Perhaps we can yet change the meaning of the saying "As goes Walmart so goes the economy"!

Consequences

Keep in mind that wage theft and wage depression are serious matters with huge ramifications. Destroying the value of work not only destroys the economic foundations of working people, it also destroys our communities, our families, our personal dispositions, as well as our faith, hope and spirits. Psychologists are beginning to examine the links between life under the conditions of capitalism and depression.[32]

As people are spending the bulk of their waking hours at work, what they experience there shapes their lives to the core, including their relationships and their ability to act. Dealing with work under attack has, thus, far-reaching consequences. In many ways, work becomes a matter of life and death. In the words of Bertolt Brecht, "What [crime] is the murder of a man compared to the hiring of a man"?[33] As ethicist Ken Estey has put it, "people die at work and they die because of work."[34]

The good news is that we are not dealing with natural catastrophes. Work is not losing its value and its power because of some law of nature but because it is under attack. This means that there is something that can be done about it at various levels. Organizing working people has already made a difference: wage theft is still rampant, but now there are organizations successfully reclaiming stolen wages. Moreover, many of these organizations are also working to change the laws that make wage theft easy and to move laws that help prevent it.

Wage *depression* is a more complex phenomenon, affecting most of us in one way or another. The top-down structure that allows for it is not easily overturned, but we have begun making our voices heard.

One of the most exciting developments we'll discuss in the following chapters is that broad coalitions are coming together to address these problems. Even some faith communities are joining the effort. While the first motivation of people of faith may be the moral outrage at clear violations of the law and at a fundamental lack of respect for people, the involvement of religion can also help us deal with the deeper problems that the attack on work creates.

If problems with work shape not only our bank accounts but also our politics, communities, relationships, families, and faith, we have to respond. Merely talking about wages and benefits is not enough.

Finally, the attacks on work must be seen in their broader structural context. Reflecting on the nature of work can help us understand what is really at stake in contemporary capitalist society. Too many well-meaning people complain about the unequal distribution of wealth without considering how work and production are valued, and thus how such stark disparities and inequality are produced in the first place.

If work and production are not valued appropriately, that is to say if working people are not compensated comprehensively for their work, no amount of redistribution will be able to change things in the long run. In fact, without valuing work and production, it will always seem workers want something for nothing, or as if they only want a giant welfare state.

As the following chapter will show, in reality, some far better options exist.

CHAPTER 3

From Advocacy to Deep Solidarity: Activism Reborn

Divide and Conquer

How do we employ the moral outrage over the most egregious abuses like wage theft and the most blatant forms of wage depression and lead it to the next steps? In the communities of faith, many have argued that we need to move from charity to advocacy, i.e., from helping people under pressure to speaking out for them and addressing that which pressures them. Solidarity is often understood in this way as well, as a privileged group supporting an underprivileged group. In this scenario, work and labor are still considered matters of special interest that affect only a smaller group of the population.

However, if 99 percent of us have to work for a living and if all work is under pressure in one way or another, things change. As we are beginning to realize, the neoliberal capitalist economy, where winner takes all, is putting more and more of us into the same boat: Even many middle-class people are only a few paychecks away from homelessness, work provides less and less freedom for self expression, and all of us experience the increasing pressures related to work, if not personally then through what is happening to our partners, our children, our parents, and our communities. Young people experience these tensions exponentially, and many young people of the middle class are finding themselves in a very different world than their parents, in whose basements many are being forced to live. These are the foundations for what we are calling *deep solidarity*.[1]

Deep solidarity recognizes that the system works for the few rather than for the many, and that nothing will change unless more of the many come together. Deep solidarity does not mean that we are all alike or that our differences do not matter anymore, just the opposite: deep solidarity allows us to deal with our differences more constructively and put them to work for a common cause.

When workers at the Target Corporation are seen talking to each other, they get reprimanded by management. This practice is not uncommon, as solidarity among workers can indeed generate some challenges for companies and has done so in the past. The proverbial water cooler conversations among white-collar workers, on the other hand, appear to be less of a problem, as there seem to be some unwritten rules that are followed that preclude solidarity. One of these rules, sometimes explicitly spelled out in contracts, is that relevant issues like salary and benefits are not to be discussed with coworkers.

When solidarity among working people results in formal efforts to form alliances and unions, companies often respond in drastic ways. Many hire so-called labor relations experts—less officially known as "union busters"—who are charged with diffusing these efforts. The methods used by these experts range from requiring workers to attend "captive audience" meetings and one-on-one conversations to accusations that unions are only after workers' contributions, threats, and severe last-minute interventions when a union drive appears to be successful. Unlike with union organizers, almost unlimited access to workers is granted to union busters, and dominant power is on their side.

Acts of charity and even advocacy are no match for the old strategy of divide-and-conquer when applied by corporations and their agents. What divide-and-conquer seeks to address is solidarity. When adjunct faculty at the New School University in New York City and at the Parsons School of Design, embarked on a successful unionizing campaign with the United Autoworkers, the university *administration* posted signs that read, "Are you an artist or an autoworker?" The administration felt so threatened by artists organizing with supportive autoworkers, they retaliated. It is worth noting that artists providing charity, or even speaking out in advocacy, for autoworkers would not be likely to have had the same effect.

Administrators appealing to the pride of those academic artists, who were slightly more privileged and better off than autoworkers, in an attempt to divide them from the bulk of working people actually has a long history in the United States. In seventeenth-century Virginia, black and white sharecroppers were divided and conquered when the white masters gave the white sharecroppers slightly more privileges and recognition so that white sharecroppers would identify with their white masters rather than their black colleagues. One of the roots of racism in the United States is still surprisingly effective even today. This racism disproportionately serves the white masters rather than their white servants. The truth of the matter is, of course, that in seventeenth-century Virginia, white sharecroppers and black sharecroppers shared more in common than white sharecroppers and white masters.

The solidarity of the oppressed was so threatening to white masters, they incited racism to divide and conquer. When white sharecroppers separated themselves from their black sisters and brothers, the white masters won. As a South African colleague once put it, racism is still one way in which the class struggle is being fought today. Even today racism is incited in subtle and not so subtle ways when the authority and privilege of the elites is threatened.

Over time, working people began to internalize the divide-and-conquer strategy.[2] After the Civil War and the end of slavery, black workers were kept out of many of the trades and barred by the craft unions of the AFL, even though the CIO unions supported racial minority workers.[3]

Sexism is another example of how divide-and-conquer works and how it is internalized. Women often found themselves even more segregated at the workplace than racial minorities, working in jobs where there were no male colleagues. The male-dominated unions of both the AFL and the CIO did not make serious efforts to organize women, and women often remained second-class citizens even when they were members of the racially progressive unions. In addition, women continue to be the primary caregivers at home. Women of color have a longer and deeper history of being affected by sexism than white women, as they were always more likely to participate in the labor force.[4]

Racism and sexism continued to hurt the labor movement after the 1960s had created increased awareness of these problems. In those years, the dominant powers were able to use populist ideas to suggest to white working people that their interests were challenged not by corporations and big money but by persons of other races. As a result, the pressures experienced by white workers were once again successfully deflected from the real causes.[5] Fred Rose is right when he notes that "if movements do not become aware of the unconscious ways in which they reinforce existing divisions in society, they are likely to encourage them."[6] By the same token, we might add that if movements do not become aware of the false identities, they are likely to play into the hands of the dominant powers as well.

Latent racism again split the solidarity of working people during the Great Recession, when Republican Presidential candidate John McCain presented "Joe the Plumber" to the American public. Joe, who was making about \$40,000 a year, spoke for the party that is known for being more supportive of corporations than working people.[7] Joe's prominence was linked to his whiteness, which resembled Republican presidential candidate John McCain's whiteness. And while it provided the proverbial fifteen minutes of fame to Joe, it did little else. Historically, whenever white working people like Joe have separated themselves as workers from their minority sisters and brothers, they are not the ones who benefit.

The same is true when those who consider themselves middle class fall for the divide-and-conquer strategy. Divisions between the middle and the working classes have supported the march to power of the elites in unprecedented ways.[8] While the white working class tends to identify with the white ruling class along the lines of race, the middle class additionally tends to identify with the ruling class along the lines of wealth: both identifications are mistaken, because the differences between someone making \$800,000 a year and someone making \$200,000 a year are greater than the differences between someone making \$200,000 a year and someone making \$20,000 a year. Imagine the possibilities of solidarity when the 99 percent begin to resist divide and conquer and pursue solidarity!

Advocacy and Solidarity

The weapon of divide and conquer is one of the greatest hurdles to solidarity even today, and the divisions are deeply engrained and internalized by now according to lines of race, ethnicity, gender, sexuality, and other identities. Other hurdles to solidarity may be less severe but they also need to be addressed because they prevent the 99 percent from succeeding. Well-meaning supporters of matters of worker justice often understand themselves as advocating for workers—particularly low-wage workers—but they fail to understand that they may have more in common than meets the eye. Advocacy is important work and a good start, but it is not quite the same as solidarity.

In more progressive religious circles, advocacy is often understood as an alternative to charity. This is a good move for two reasons. First, advocacy is indeed a significant improvement over charity. Charity is the well-meaning effort to help others in need, providing basic support of matters like food, shelter, care, and education. Although these forms of charity provide helpful services, they all address symptoms rather than the underlying causes. Advocacy, by contrast, is concerned about the causes of the problems that people experience.

Second, and contrary to a commonly held belief, advocacy is more deeply rooted in many faith traditions than charity. While large numbers of people of faith assume that charity is the most faithful response to social problems, there are other responses that are equally or even more faithful yet. Many of the prophets of the Hebrew Bible (Jews call it the Tanakh[9]), also recognized in Christianity and with some resonances in Islam, speak out against the injustices that oppress the poor and other marginalized groups like widows, orphans, and strangers.

Like other prophets, Amos condemns those who "trample on the poor and take from them levies of grain" (Amos 5:11). In Christianity, Jesus speaks out against oppressive customs that put pressures on the poor, women, children, and those who are sick and thus excluded from the community. Jesus preaches good news to the poor, not charity: receiving handouts is not good news to the poor; being no longer poor is (Matt. 11:5; Luke 4:18). Standing in this tradition, John Wesley, the founder of Methodism in the eighteenth century, proclaimed that the majority of people were poor not by their own fault but because they were pushed from their lands by wealthy landowners and then exploited in the factories of early capitalism.[10]

When dealing with poverty, for instance, advocates are not blaming the poor for their misery, and neither are they simply trying to provide services to poor people; rather, advocates seek to address and bring to an end the conditions that cause poverty. Instead of blaming low-wage workers for their inability to make ends meet, for instance, advocates speak out for the need to raise the minimum wage and to establish a living wage that allows workers and their families to make ends meet.

Since advocacy often brings us closer to the core of the problem than charity, pushback is to be expected. Dom Hélder Câmara, a Brazilian bishop, once put it like this: "When I give food to the poor, they call me a saint. When I ask why they are poor, they call me a communist."[11] Pushback, while not something that most people enjoy, is often a sign that we are on the right track. The ministry of the prophets, of Jesus, and of Muhammad demonstrates this: only the false prophets and the false messiahs go unchallenged.

Deep Solidarity

Solidarity, and deep solidarity in particular pushes us one more step beyond advocacy. Advocacy quickly reaches its limits when advocates fail to understand their deep connections with those for whom they are advocating. Too many advocates assume that they are somehow above or unaffected by the problem, merely wanting to help others who are less fortunate. The same is true for some forms of solidarity. In the past, solidarity has sometimes been misunderstood as the privileged supporting the underprivileged. Well-meaning people in the countries of the global North, for instance, have at times declared their solidarity with people in the countries of the global South, without understanding what they share in common.[12] This pattern has been especially prevalent in religious communities.

One-sided solidarity, while well meaning and sincerely trying to help, creates several problems. One is those who consider themselves privileged are calling the shots, acting as if they had the ability to fix the problems alone. This rarely works, because the problems are usually too big and because the privileged group is not able to understand what is going on without those who are most immediately affected. Another problem has to do with the fact that those who consider themselves privileged feel like they can walk away from solidarity whenever they had enough because they fail to understand the deeper connections.

We are using the term "deep solidarity" to address these problems and to suggest a better way forward. Deep solidarity describes a situation where the 99 percent of us who have to work for a living develop some understanding that we are in the same boat. The question is not just, as one Christian theologian put it, "How can the church maintain integrity in its relationship with workers?"[13] The question is how faith communities can begin to understand that they are mostly made up of working people, that most of us are workers now, and that even what is considered divine joins us in deep solidarity. Other communities, including the unions and their supporters, can benefit from this perspective as well. To be sure, understanding our deep connections and relationships does not mean that our differences have to be covered up. Just the opposite: deep solidarity allows us to respect our differences and to put them to productive use.

Deep solidarity is possible when the 99 percent realize that most of us benefit less and less from the current economic situation. This includes those who consider themselves middle class or somewhat privileged. As the fortunes of the 1 percent are growing, the middle class is less and less able to keep up, faced with increasing college costs for the next generation that may not even find jobs, reduction of benefits and job security, reduction of social security, ever more limited healthcare plans, and an increasingly obvious loss of political power.

In terms of simple math, someone who earns $150,000 a year is closer to someone who earns $15,000 a year than to someone who earns $500,000 a year—the realm where membership in the 1 percent barely begins. Earnings are, of course, merely the tip of the iceberg. What matters is power. Even members of the middle class, including the ones who feel fairly comfortable at the moment, have surprisingly little power over their future: they cannot do much to push back when the corporation requires them to work harder and longer hours, they cannot do much to secure their personal investments, which are subject to ever greater market fluctuations from which mostly the insiders benefit, and they cannot do a whole lot to truly secure their future.

Perhaps most important of all is that the middle class can no longer assume that the next generation will still be middle class or better, the foundation of the American Dream which is intergenerational. Even members of the middle class cannot do much if their children move back home when they fail to get jobs after college, a reality that affects more and more families even outside of regularly occurring recessions. The younger generations who are forced to go into debt, with greatly reduced expectations of reward, understand these problems even more clearly. It is not surprising that this generation stepped up to the plate during the heyday of the Occupy Wall Street movement, pointing out the difference between the 1 percent and the 99 percent unlike any other generation before.

"As goes Walmart so goes the economy," we stated earlier. This is true at the level of work itself, as even the better jobs are becoming more and more precarious, with the potential of being cut at any time. Today, white-collar workers are often just as affected as blue-collar workers by the corporate efforts to maximize profits at all costs. The proletariat of working people is turning into what some have called the "precariat," a diverse group of working people that includes a cross section of the 99 percent who are forced to bear the brunt of increasing insecurity, risk, and pressure at work.[14] Whenever jobs are cut, the jobs that are coming back are designed for temp workers, workers without benefits, and those who are willing to work for less.

Unfortunately, what happens at the level of work and labor also happens in every other area of life. Like the members of the working-class majority (at 63 percent of the population), members of the middle class (at 35 percent of the population) have less and less power in their communities, whereas the larger donors and philanthropists call the shots in cities and towns, as well as religious communities. Influencing elections at the regional, state, and national levels is completely out of the reach of individual members of the working and middle classes.

In other words, the middle class finds itself closer to the working class and the poor than ever before. In this climate, solidarity is no longer a matter of the privileged helping the underprivileged; rather, solidarity is a matter of understanding what we have in common and that we need to work together if we want to make a difference not only at work but in any other area of life. For the 99 percent working majority, trying to replicate the power of the 1 percent is not an option. We will never be able to beat them at their game: the gap is simply too vast. Of course, there are differences with the top 1 percent as well, as the difference between millions and billions is much more difficult to grasp than most people realize.[15] It is very hard to comprehend in financial terms that one family can own as much as 42 percent of all Americans combined; it is almost impossible to comprehend what that difference means in terms of power and influence.[16] As stated above, even in the Roman Empire the top 1 percent controlled only 16 percent of all wealth.

Not all is lost, however. To the contrary: these sharp differences can help us to develop an understanding of what the rest of us have in common, to resist divide-and-conquer, and to reconnect that which belongs together. In the process, we can learn to develop different forms of power, which are not only more powerful than the power of the 1 percent but also longer-lasting. Deep solidarity, it seems to us, has the power to make a real difference.

Ancient Stories of Deep Solidarity

Such deep solidarity is embodied by some of the key figures of our faith. Mary, the mother of Jesus, is often portrayed as a privileged person, wearing the clothes of nobility and a crown. In real life, she was a common person—an unwed mother who later married a construction worker—and there is no indication that she ever joined the 1 percent. Mary is aware that God chose her to be the mother of Jesus not because she was better than others; by choosing her, God lifted up the lowly, she states (Luke 1:48, 52). In the Bible, Mary not only praises God for lifting up the lowly; she also celebrates the fact that the God who lifts up the lowly pushes the powerful from their thrones and fills the hungry with good things while sending the rich away empty (Luke 1:52–53).

Mary thus joins God in deep solidarity with those who are pushed to the ground, celebrating a new day in organizing. Who knows, the powerful who are being pushed from their thrones and the rich who are sent away empty might appreciate the opportunity to join the emerging deep solidarity as well.

Another story of deep solidarity that is shared by Jews, Christians, and Muslims, is the story of Moses in the Exodus from Egypt. As the ancient traditions tell us, Moses was a descendant of the Hebrew slaves who was raised as an Egyptian Prince in Pharaoh's court. Things change, however, when he sees the Hebrew slaves being mistreated. According to the book of Exodus, Moses overreacts and kills one of the Egyptian slave masters. This act certainly does not make Moses a leader, even in the eyes of the Hebrew slaves, who challenge his action (Ex. 2:11–14). In exile, Moses learns to live the life of a worker and it takes years before he moves to the next step, developing the skills of an organizer in collaboration with his brother Aaron and his sister Miriam.[17] Since Moses finds it difficult to speak, Aaron becomes the spokesperson of the movement, who tells Pharaoh to let the Israelites go. Miriam, who is also called a prophet, is a popular leader a well (Ex.15:20–21).

The ancient story of the burning bush is instructive for our reflections on deep solidarity. In this story, God speaks to Moses out of a bush that is burning but is not consumed. While this miracle is often noted and remembered, the actual speech is not. It bears quoting here. God said to Moses:

> I have observed the misery of my people who are in Egypt; I have heard their cry on account of their taskmasters. Indeed, I know their sufferings, and I have come down to deliver them from the Egyptians, and to bring them up out of that land to a good and broad land, a land flowing with milk and honey, to the country of the Canaanites, the Hittites, the Amorites, the Perizzites, the Hivites, and the Jebusites. The cry of the Israelites has now come to me; I have also seen how the Egyptians oppress them. So come, I will send you to Pharaoh to bring my people, the Israelites, out of Egypt. (Ex.3:7–10).

Deep solidarity is expressed in this passage first of all in God's own actions. While there is no explanation for why it may have taken God so long to notice the struggles of the Hebrew slaves, God now speaks of seeing and hearing what is going on as the Egyptian slave masters wage class struggle against the Hebrews. What is more, God decides to join the struggle for liberation. Moses, the shepherd of his father-in-law's flock, having long abandoned his status as a prince in Egypt, now joins the struggles of his people in Egypt under the leadership of a God who is committed to taking sides. Both men and women collaborate in the movement, even though Miriam only gets short mention in the texts, which were probably written by men.

And while the Exodus seems to end in another conquest—that of the Promised Land—some scholars have argued that the Hebrew tribes entered into solidarity with oppressed groups there and challenged the powers in the dominant city-states that oppressed the rural populations.[18] This would constitute yet another example of deep solidarity.

Deep solidarity opens up a window on who God is in the Abrahamic religions: in the Exodus stories, God is not working from the outside, as the models of charity and advocacy often assume; rather, God is part of the struggle and God takes sides. This is made clear also in the references to the Exodus in the Qur'an in Surah 26, particularly in the passage through the sea 26:61–68.

Nevertheless, the dominant powers are not pushed aside here but called to conversion and repentance. Even Pharaoh gets several chances ("let my people go," Exodus 5:1, 7:16, 8:1, etc.; see also Qur'an 7:105).[19] In some cases, the 1 percent decide to join the 99 percent working majority, even though this does not happen in the Exodus story.

Deep solidarity is also expressed in the life of Jesus of Nazareth. He grew up as a carpenter—as the Greek term *tektōn* is usually translated. This means that Jesus was what today we would call a construction worker, working with whatever building materials were at hand, including wood and stone. As a construction worker, he was most likely also part of trade associations that were widespread in the Ancient world.[20] In the Roman Empire, construction workers were often hired for the large building projects, where they would have experienced conditions that many construction workers experience today, including long working hours, lack of water and safety equipment, and no benefits. When the jobs were finished, most of these workers would be laid off. It is, therefore, very likely that Jesus and his family would have experienced unemployment as well.

Jesus embodies deep solidarity not merely because he grew up as a worker but because he never made any efforts to move "up and out." To the contrary, he stayed in deep solidarity with working people his whole life. His birth was first witnessed by shepherds—day laborers who tended someone else's flock. Many of his disciples were working people. Even though most of their professions are unknown, we know that four of them (Peter, Andrew, James, and John) were fishermen. Jesus's parables are full of examples from everyday labor and work, telling the stories of shepherds, who usually were not the owners of their flocks, of working women, of workers in vineyards and in fields, of fishermen, and of service workers.

That one of Jesus's disciples, Matthew, reportedly was a tax collector further affirms what we mean by deep solidarity. If he was a member of the 99 percent, as many scholars argue, Matthew realized his deep connectedness to the common people who made up the Jesus movement. If he was a member of the 1 percent, Matthew shows that the 1 percent can indeed join the solidarity of the 99 percent and that true conversion is possible. In either case, what is very clear is that Matthew and other privileged people who were part of the Jesus movement did not convert Jesus to the 1 percent; the opposite is the case: Jesus converted them to join the 99 percent.

Then as now, the 99 percent were not always a unified force, and divide and conquer was a method commonly employed. Jesus's well-known admonition to love one's enemies (Matt. 5:44) is best understood in this context, as an effort to bring together local communities that were divided and who would benefit from supporting each other and being in solidarity.[21]

Deep solidarity was not restricted to the 99 percent. Several wealthy and prominent women who followed Jesus (Luke 8:1–3), as well as Zacchaeus, a prominent tax collector who may have been a 1 percenter (Luke 19:1–10), also embody it as well. When Zacchaeus, after his encounter with Jesus, turns over half of his wealth to the poor and makes four-fold restitution to those whom he defrauded, he is not merely engaging in charity but joins in deep solidarity with those who are trampled underfoot in the Roman Empire: working people, peasants, and the unemployed. It is not hard to imagine the consequences of this public stand of solidarity. The solidarity of the powerful, with whom Zacchaeus was connected before he met Jesus, is now no longer available to him. The same is most likely true for the wealthy women who joined Jesus. Imagine the consequences when Joanna, the wife of one of King Herod's officials, began supporting the Jesus movement (Luke 8:2-3)!

The culmination of Jesus' message might be considered preaching good news to the poor (referenced several times in the gospels, for instance Matthew 11 and Luke 4). Preaching good news to the poor leads to questions like, Who "tramples on the poor" (Amos) and on working people today? Who "takes from them levies of grain" (Amos again), including fair wages and benefits? The only good news to the poor is that they will no longer be poor—feel-good messages, pie-in-the-sky calls for perseverance, and even handouts are not enough.

While deep solidarity demands challenging those who harm working people, its deepest concern is the positive transformation of society and the creation of new community.[22]

The Resilience of Deep Solidarity

To be sure, presenting challenges and real alternatives was never easy, and there are consequences. According to the Gospel of Luke, Jesus's first proclamation of good news to the poor ended with an attempt by the faith community to throw him off a cliff (Luke 4:16–30). What seems to have enraged the community in particular was that Jesus claimed that he would be the one bringing the good news.

Had Jesus merely intended to be a heroic advocate for the poor without working toward deep solidarity, his claim would have indeed been arrogant or even blasphemous. Moreover, without working towards deep solidarity, his movement might have ended abruptly if they had managed to throw him off that cliff in Nazareth; or else it would have ended later at the point of his crucifixion. However we interpret Jesus's story here, the reality of pushback highlights the limits of advocacy and the need for deep solidarity.

The two biggest drawbacks of advocacy are, first, that advocates often stifle the agency of those for whom they speak and, second, that advocates often overestimate their own power. The dominant powers benefit from both moves. Jesus would have scarcely been a threat to the Roman Empire of his times if he had acted alone or with a select group of radicals. And Jesus would not have been a threat had he assumed that he could do this work all by himself, like an ancient superhero, following the models of Superman, Spiderman, or Batman. The same is true for individual organizations or small groups of people who refuse to be in solidarity with other groups or broader movements, no matter how committed or radical they might be.

Working people, the 99 percent who work for a living, will not be able to make a difference if they assume that the support of a few advocates will do the trick. Elected officials, sympathetic 1 percenters, and a couple of well-meaning nonprofit organizations can make some difference, but they will not be able to turn the tide. Deep solidarity requires us to think about the agency of all of us and what contributions we can make to the common good together.

This has wide-reaching implications for how we understand democracy both in politics and economics. In the model of deep solidarity, elected officials, for instance, are no longer the agents of working people; rather, they are working alongside working people, putting their powers and authority to use in this context. Enlightened business leaders no longer have to guess what people might need; rather, by working alongside working people they can put their abilities to use in ways that directly improve the lives of workers and their communities.

The second problem, that advocates tend to overestimate their own power, is equally significant. Rarely are the dominant powers challenged by a few prominent voices. This is why these dominant powers want to have us believe that individuals like Martin Luther King Jr., or Rosa Parks acted singlehandedly. If Rosa Parks were merely some woman who at some point got tired of segregation in public transportation and sat down in the wrong section of a bus, her acts are heroic but not dangerous. If a pastor, however eloquent or prominent, preaches a good sermon, his act may be heroic but it is hardly dangerous either, without the support of a broader community that is well organized and active.

White males who enjoy some privileges in particular often overestimate their own power. We tend to assume that people are actually listening to what we have to say and that when we stand up and make demands or issue calls to action, things will change. Such advocacy is doomed to failure because the dominant system will not be impressed by a few dissidents, even if they band together in small groups. Warren Buffett, one of the richest individuals on the planet, may serve as an example. When Buffett speaks in the name of top investors, his advice is heeded and people act accordingly; this is what happens when the privileged join their power with that of the dominant system. However, when Buffett warns of the consequences of the class struggle, as he has done repeatedly, he is but a lone voice crying in the wilderness.[23]

Power that works based on the system cannot easily be transferred to alternative kinds of power. Trying to use dominant power and privilege for other purposes usually ends in failure. At the systemic level (whether in economics, politics, or religion), whatever alternative emerges, it is quickly subsumed by the dominant powers. At the personal level, the failure to produce true and lasting change leads to resignation and burnout. Examples can be given for both cases. Consider, for instance, the efforts of a regional organization of churches to "eradicate poverty" in two different zip codes. It is impossible to eradicate poverty without addressing what caused it in the first place (asset poverty, for instance, is hardly a cause but a symptom of poverty); trying to harness the dominant powers to clean up the mess that they created will not very likely lead to success. Moreover, those who are charged with making it happen will not only experience frustration but may be burdened with blame that is easily internalized; burnout unfortunately is very common.

Deep solidarity is necessary to deal with these problems. Rosa Parks, for instance, in addition to being a person of great courage, was trained by the civil rights movement and prepared for the role that she would eventually play in the Montgomery Bus Boycott. By the same token, Martin Luther King Jr., did not invent or start the civil rights movement; rather, King acted in deep solidarity with many grassroots groups that emerged all over the country in diverse locations linked to diverse organizations. This is why with the shooting of King the movement did not end, as many had undoubtedly hoped. Despite the shock and the deep depression King's murder caused, things continued to move ahead.

Deep solidarity helps us overcome roadblocks, including the divide and conquer efforts of the system. It is based on an understanding that those of us who have to work for a living, the 99 percent working majority, have a great deal in common. We find ourselves in the same boat, however, not because we are all alike and our differences do not matter; rather, we find ourselves in the same boat because of the dominant system and its efforts to use all of our work and labor for the accumulation of profit and gain at the very top.

The clearer we are about this the more deep solidarity becomes an option. Work and labor are what connects us, up and down the various social ladders and scales that exist among the 99 percent.[24] Deep solidarity is built on the awareness that we are all working people now—including the underemployed and the unemployed, the vast majority of whom would much rather work than sit idle and wait for handouts.

Valuing Diversity and Putting it to Use

Solidarity that is restricted to some limited group is often counterproductive. In the case of the solidarity of work and labor, as economist Marcellus Andrews has pointed out, capitalist competition does not mind narrow labor solidarity.[25] Narrow labor solidarity is self-defeating because it gets pulled into the competitive game. Whatever success a small group achieves for itself will be undermined by those who are left out, whose anger and frustration is useful to the dominant system. As a result, we agree with Andrews that "narrow labor solidarity is no solidarity at all, but instead a road to enduring racial hatred and broad labor weakness."[26]

Deep solidarity is anything but narrow. One of its most important traits is that it does not require us to be alike or set our differences aside.[27] Just the opposite: deep solidarity benefits from our differences brought together for the common good. Deep solidarity develops power by putting our differences to productive use while deconstructing their negative aspects. Moreover, as we put our differences to use, we begin to realize that those who are forced to endure the greatest pressures might have the most valuable lessons to teach.

Deep solidarity not only thrives on differences, it also brings to light otherwise hidden privileges and helps deconstruct them.[28] The world of working people and labor is one of the best places to start. As W. E. B. Du Bois has observed: "Probably the greatest and most effective effort toward interracial understanding among the working masses has come about through the trade unions."[29] From the religious side, Dorothy Day, cofounder of the *Catholic Worker* newspaper might be seen as embodying such deep solidarity. College-educated, she noted in conversation with a group of Harvard students toward the end of her life: "We've been given a leg up in the world, so why not try to help others get a bit of a break, too?"[30] What if these were not the condescending words of a 1 percenter but those of a participant who recognizes limited privilege and begins to deconstruct it? Day, after all, lived with workers and organized with them, from the bottom up.

The tensions of race and ethnicity may serve as our first example. Becoming aware of deep solidarity as working people, white people begin to understand that they may have more in common with so-called racial and ethnic minorities than with white elites. The advantages that white working people enjoy in comparison to their minority colleagues may be significant, but they pale in comparison to the advantages that the white elites enjoy over white workers. White employees may indeed have the ear of white employers, receive slightly better salaries and benefits than African American, Hispanic, or Asian employees, and are more likely to get hired to scarce job openings. Nevertheless, their whiteness still does not put them on par with their employers. White workers, like other workers, are hardly able to challenge and confront their superiors on matters of consequence. And while it is true that white people can expect to be treated better when shopping at the mall, whites who belong to the elites have an entirely different relationship to their suppliers than the rest of us.

In this situation, an awareness of deep solidarity can provide white people with an opportunity to use whatever power they may have differently. White workers who have more clout with their bosses can use it in alternative fashion, for instance by putting in a good word for others or by speaking up when nobody expects it. White shoppers who are more valued have a choice either to conform or to challenge the places they frequent and to let employers know that they are paying attention to how employees are treated. In the process, the power of the 99 percent increases when white working people begin to talk to each other and to others with whom they would usually not be in contact. And power is built when white working people begin to listen to other working people who, because they are forced to endure even greater pressures, might be able to see more clearly not only the problems but also the possibilities.

Using one's limited privilege differently may be the best way to deconstruct it. White power is deconstructed when white working people begin to question their ties with dominant white power and put whatever privilege they have in the service of deep solidarity with their fellow workers of racial and ethnic minorities. Feeling guilty about one's privilege on the other hand—a common response when people become aware of it—prevents its productive use altogether. While white working people should not overestimate their own power—the whiteness of a worker by itself will not win the battle—underestimating it would also be a mistake.

What about gender relationships? In 2013, women were paid 78 cents of every dollar a white man earns doing the same work, Asian American women 90 cents, African American women 64 cents, American Indian (and Alaska Native) women 59 cents, and Latina women 54 cents.[31] In addition, women earn only 38 percent of what men earn during their prime working years between 26–59. As Christian ethicist Melissa Snarr has pointed out, these experiences make women's leadership in living wage coalitions particularly valuable, especially when considering that women are often less politically active than men and view themselves as less influential than men.[32] Deep solidarity for men, in this case, means to understand how their fate is actually connected more closely to women than to men of the elite groups. While a man in a heterosexual marriage may get some benefits out of being a macho or a patriarch at home, he might benefit a good deal more if the work of wife were to be valued by a decent income and if solidarity led her to activate her own powers for the common good. When relating to women in these new ways, men can learn how to use whatever power they have in a patriarchal world to challenge the dominant powers. This is how patriarchal power is deconstructed. Some feminist theologians have made this argument about Jesus's ways of being a man: the fact that a man spoke out against patriarchal power and in support of women must have come as a surprise, as men are expected to support other men. The dominant system was certainly not anticipating this, and neither were some of Jesus's closest followers, but this is precisely why it made a difference.[33] The women of the Jesus movement, unlike the men, seemed to have learned more quickly and took on positions of leadership. [34] This reversal of leadership is taking place not only in certain communities of faith but also in some labor unions; men do well to listen to women. Of course, using male privilege against patriarchy means to lose it eventually, as the good old boys will not easily forgive and forget.

It should be noted that the unions have made some progress in these areas in recent decades, as the leadership of women and minorities has grown stronger. While in the late 1980s merely 12 percent of women and 15 percent of racial minorities were lead organizers, in 2005 that number had grown to 21 percent women and 22 percent racial minorities; women of racial minority groups now make up 7 percent of lead organizers.[35] In addition, union contracts now increasingly reference sexual orientation as a characteristic against which employers cannot discriminate.[36]

When race, ethnicity, gender, and sexuality come together, matters become more complex yet. Deep solidarity in these relationships can only be forged if it becomes clear how the work and labor of all of us are under pressure, although the work of some more than others. When jobs are sent overseas, for instance, the racism that is sometimes part of this move and that endorses treating nonwhites and particularly women in other countries less well, also hurts white male workers in the United States. Likewise, when during the Great Recession men were sometimes laid off before women, the sexism in this move as women provide cheaper labor then men, ends up hurting men as well.

Deep solidarity in these cases can prevent us from blaming the victims (international workers and women), identify where energy and agency are found, and direct our agency to where it can make a difference. Among organizing poultry workers in the South of the United States, for instance, African American workers were in a better position (due to their traditions and their citizenship) to speak out against unfair labor practices when compared with immigrant workers from south of the border, which made multiracial and ethnic dialogues essential.[37] While many white American men who belong to the 99 percent working majority still need to learn some painful lessons about the limits of their power, they can now employ their limited power in such a way that the community benefits rather than the elites.

For relatively privileged members of the middle class who have to work for a living, everything changes when they become aware of deep solidarity. Now they can put some of their privileges to use so that they will actually make a difference, reshaping their identity in the process. Instead of using their education for shoring up the position of the 1 percent, college-educated people can now put their expertise and their knowledge to work for the well-being of the 99 percent. All areas and fields of study are useful: how do we assess the current political, financial, psychological, social, cultural, scientific, and religious situations? What alternatives might there be when these inequities sink in and a substantial number of people shift their allegiances?

Still, the middle class will not be able to do any of this without the input and guidance of those who are less privileged. While deep solidarity reminds us that we are in the same boat, we should never forget that some are worse off than others. Those who feel the pressures of the system most acutely are the ones who have no reserves, who financially depend almost exclusively on their income from work, and who are therefore predisposed to see and feel more clearly what is going on.

Deep solidarity that puts diversity to work gets a boost when we look at it from the perspective of work and labor. Here is where everything comes together: race, ethnicity, gender, sexuality, age, etc. The need to work for a living ties us into concerns of many of the popular movements, including the Occupy Wall Street movement—realizing the fundamental difference between the 1 percent and the 99 percent—and the Black Lives Matter movement—as black lives are destroyed in ways that include what is happening at work or in the lack of work. Even human trafficking, perhaps one of the most heinous crimes of our time, is tied to work, as most human trafficking turns out to be labor trafficking. Likewise, wage theft and the lowest rungs of wage depression are often tied to racism, ethnocentrism, and sexism.

In this light, deep solidarity becomes a matter of life and death. Here is where we might find the power and the energy to make a difference and to preserve life. Work, because of the fact that we are spending too much time at it and that its pressures affect us more deeply than we ever imagined, welds us together at many levels. Minds, hearts, and bodies are all involved. As one of my graduate students, Ben Robinson, put it: "We may march together, we may work together, but we are not in solidarity until we *feel* together."[38]

Deep solidarity, to recap, helps us to take into account and make use of the fact that the 99 percent have more in common with each other than with the 1 percent. This allows for more effective action and collaboration without erasing differences. As we recognize our deep connectedness linked to work, work assumes the transformative character indicated in the introduction. Political, economic, and religious activism is part of our everyday work rather than something that belongs to leisure time, as this activism is informed and energized by our work. Both the pressures and the potential of work matter.

While the 99 percent working majority are together in this, whether they are aware of it or not, it is not necessary to expect that everybody will join us. In fact, because things are urgent, it would not be wise to waste too much time on those who are not ready yet. Instead, we need to connect with those growing numbers of people who are waking up every day, realizing that they have less and less power in their jobs and their lives. These people come from all walks of life, from various races, genders, sexualities, from farmworkers toiling in the hot sun all day to lawyers slaving away for billable hours. A certain critical mass is needed for change to happen, of course, but it will not take 99 percent of the 99 percent.

The best news yet is that deep solidarity does not have to be produced artificially. Deep solidarity is not primarily about a moral exhortation to work together: it is about finding common roots in our experiences as working people, both positively and negatively. As a result, all we need to do is help people deepen their budding senses of what is going on and that we find ourselves in the same boat, whether we are aware of it at first or not. Our task is simple when it comes to deep solidarity: become aware of it, experiment with it, explore it at various levels, and above all resist any efforts to be divided and conquered once again.

CHAPTER 4

Labor Radicalizing Religion

Two Dying Institutions?

When some time ago Joerg mentioned to an experienced labor organizer that his work brings together labor and religion, her flippant response was, "Good luck! You are dealing with two dying institutions!" While we never had any illusions that this project would be easy, we nevertheless see some hope on the horizon. Labor has picked up some steam, with 58 percent of Americans approving of labor unions.[1] Labor is growing again particularly in Southern states like Texas where no one would have expected it. And even though the mainline churches are in decline, religion continues to enjoy a lot of clout in the United States. There is even some hope for progressive religion, it seems to us, but progress will only be made if religion and labor work together again, as they have at various times in the past.[2] One needs the other, not just for pragmatic reasons but because of some very deep connections.

It is well known that in polite conversation the topics of politics and religion should never be mentioned. This is true to an even greater degree for the topic of labor. There are good reasons for these taboos. Disagreements on topics of politics, religion, and labor are passionate, so that the subjects can quickly ruin a polite conversation. These topics are touchy not just because people tend to disagree on them but also because they touch on the basic issues of life. Our most basic commitments and beliefs are tied up with politics, religion, and labor.

Of course, neither labor nor religion ever made much progress by observing the taboos of dominant society. While current efforts of labor and religion to adapt to the status quo are understandable, tied to concerns that some embodiments of labor and of religion are indeed dying today, they do not seem the right way forward. So, we may be better off addressing these topics head on and dealing with them, even if it might make some of us uncomfortable.

Scholars of religion have long sought to understand what is at the core of religion, and one of the definitions given is the "ultimate concern."[3] Topics like politics and labor, while crucially important to our lives, usually do not claim the status of ultimate concerns. But what if this were a mistake? What if matters of labor, for instance, are indeed matters of ultimate concern? If we are spending most of our waking hours at work, rather than with our families or engaged in what is considered "religious practice," does this not mean that at least we're tacitly conceding that labor is actually what concerns us most, whether we admit it or not?

Considering work and labor as ultimate concerns may sound odd, but in capitalist societies, people define themselves by the work they do. While organized labor is not part of polite conversation, the question "what do you do (for a living)?" is one of the most common questions at social events of the middle class, and what we do for a living shapes us all the way down, providing the backbone to even our most intimate relationships. This is true even in European countries where people work fewer hours than in the United States and enjoy six or eight weeks of vacation from work each year.

Thinking about labor and religion together, therefore, makes a great deal of sense. Summarizing what we have covered so far, we can say: 1. Labor is central to our lives but widely ignored or covered up; 2. Labor affects everything and shapes us all the way down; 3. Labor brings together the vital concerns of gender, race, and class; 4. Labor helps us create new solidarity. As a next step, we will talk about how labor helps us radicalize religion.

Keep in mind that radicalizing literally means going back to the roots of something. The Latin word *radix* means root. To radicalize does not mean to go wild or to go over the top, as those who prefer the safety and comfort of the middle road tend to assume. To radicalize, in the sense we are using the word, means to reclaim our roots, to take them seriously, and to see what difference this might make.

The Problem of Religion

Despite many predictions, religion has not disappeared in the twenty-first century. Religion has fared worse in some of the European countries where it openly sided with the elites against working people. In the United States and many other countries, on the other hand, religion is embraced by many working people as well. This is particularly true in the Southern regions of the United States, where the majority of the population is actively affiliated with religious communities. At a recent gathering of five hundred union leaders in Dallas, Texas, more than four hundred raised their hands when asked whether they were affiliated with religious communities.

Religion is a powerful reality, for good or for ill, that needs to be taken into account. This fact is increasingly recognized by progressives as well, as parts of religion have shown support for labor, for women, for racial, ethnic, and sexual minorities, and for the environment. The "Southern Strategy" pronounced by the AFL-CIO in 2013 includes efforts to take religion more seriously as a labor ally with much to contribute to the common good.

To be sure, the popularity of religion among the Southern working majority does not automatically make it an ally. Despite deep affinities of religion and labor, which are the subject of this chapter, religion has often been used against working people. Different streams are pushing against us, sometimes combining forces. The following observations are not offered from the outside; we are looking at religion from the inside, as people deeply shaped by religion and involved in its practices.

One understanding of religion that is rooted in modern political and philosophical developments considers religion as mostly an otherworldly affair that is limited to the private lives of individuals. This understanding of religion may seem harmless at first, but it directs people's energies and attentions away from real-life issues. Growing up in a Methodist family in Germany, with his parents and grandparents members of the postal workers union, Joerg vividly remember the conflicts this narrow understanding of religion produced: while his parents were leaders both in the church and in the union, the church always had priority. While this may not be a problem in itself, in this case the church prevented them from realizing the broader implications of their faith for the community and from developing more appropriate images of God that would incorporate their involvement in matters of labor.

Another problem with religion is that God is often envisioned as a person exercising top-down power, like the kings in the days of old or like a boss today. This seems like a logical conclusion since people of faith believe that God has great power, to the point of being omnipotent—all powerful. What is overlooked here, however, is that in various religious traditions God's power is presented in different ways. A search for the notion of God as king in the Bible produces surprisingly few results.[4] In some cases, God is portrayed as opposing the power of kings because of the exploitation and oppression that so often goes with the office. Jews and

Christians share these traditions.[5] In other cases, God's power is at work in the people rather than in the elites. We will have to take a closer look at these questions momentarily.

Another problem with religion today is what has become known as the "gospel of prosperity." Here, religion promises people fantastic wealth and success in exchange for obedience to certain ideas and principles. Some assume that this is in the interest of working people. After all, are working people not also striving for better lives, for the ability to make ends meet, and to live the good life before they die? The problem with the gospel of prosperity, however, is that it envisions God in the image of the elites, an image that is not helpful to the working majority.

Envisioning God as a 1 percenter and celebrating those in the community who have made it up the ladder of power and wealth covers up the fact that this is not an option for the majority of people. The gospel of prosperity is not a program that lifts up the working majority or raises the poor out of poverty; almost like the lottery, it empowers a few and leaves the rest hoping for success that will never happen. And worse than the lottery: the masses left behind have no one but themselves to blame.

Religion can help provide lifelines for working people that 1 percenters do not need. Unfortunately, it is for this reason that working people are also more likely to be fooled and played by religion. In the United States, unlike in Europe, working people are more likely to be in church and they contribute a higher percentage of their income to others.[6]

Reclaiming Ancient Traditions

When seen through the lenses of work and labor, religion shapes up differently. Religion does not have to be limited to endeavors in otherworldly imagination or turned into mind games that preserve the values of the elites. When put in touch with the issues of real life, religion returns to its sources. In many cases the sources and origins of religion are linked to the lives of ordinary working people in various walks of life. Religion appears to be at its best when it is located in the communal struggles of everyday life, where God is found to be at work.

The three Abrahamic religions have their beginnings in the struggle for liberation of the Hebrew slaves in Egypt, in which God joins. In the traditions of Judaism, Christianity, and Islam, Godself is presented not as a manager but as a worker who forms the human being from the dust of the ground (Gen. 2:7, Qur'an 15.26, 15.28) and plants a garden (Gen. 2:8–9). God goes about the creation of the world just as working people would do, rather than as a supervisor or a boss. This is in diametrical opposition to other ancient traditions, where the gods create humans in order to work and to assure divine leisure.[7] There are other traditions in the Bible where God's act of creating is seen as less hands-on (Gen.1:1—2:3), but by no means does this erase the traditions of God as worker and the value of work. In Genesis 2:2, God rests from work after six days, a gesture which has been an inspiration for working people through the ages.

The majority of the Christian traditions go one step further yet when they hold that God joined the workforce as a day laborer in construction in the incarnation of Jesus Christ. Since there would have been other options—Christ could have been born into the family of the high priests in Jerusalem or the royals related to the Roman Empire— this matter is much more significant than is commonly acknowledged.

Christians who believe that Jesus Christ is both fully human and fully divine have to deal with an image of God in Christ that does not easily fit in with widely held ideas of God as a monarch or as a heavenly boss. As some of the ancient Christian traditions state, Jesus Christ is of the same substance as God, and there is no subordination of one under the other, no before and no after, and no separation of the two.[8] As a result, Christian images of God tie into the reality of working people in very special ways. The realities of work and labor can help Christians recover these images, which have often been repressed.

Unfortunately, most faith communities are unaware of the deep implications of these and other religious traditions that tie religion to the everyday life of working people. Instead, religions have been lured into understanding themselves as matters of otherworldly affairs, having mostly to do with another world or with private affairs. In the process, religion has lost most of its meaning and almost all of its bite. So great is the confusion that many people of faith tend to assume that religion equals religious ritual and cult—whatever happens on one of the days of the weekend, depending on what days different religious groups meet for worship. No wonder that many people are losing interest in religion today.

Yet few of the key figures of the Abrahamic religions spent the bulk of their time in worship or dealing with matters of religion in the narrow sense.[9] Abraham, Moses, the prophets, Jesus, Muhammad, and the later Jewish rabbis were down-to-earth people who were interested in the well-being of their communities and in how relationships with God shape up in relation to other human beings. All of them were concerned with how faith transforms the world. This is true even for supposedly more ethereal figures like the apostle Paul and the various mystics, as we are beginning to understand. Paul's message was grounded in an alternative way of life in the midst of the Roman Empire. The same is true for many of the mystics of various religious traditions, both women and men: they were not just dreamers and visionaries, their visions were grounded in alternative ways of life as well. In Buddhism, for instance, this can be seen in the representatives of Engaged Buddhism, who bring together meditation and action.[10]

The Promise of Religion

Encounters with the world of labor can help people of all faiths rediscover these ancient wisdom traditions and reclaim them. The implications for religious communities of these encounters of religion and labor go far beyond the projects of charity, social service, and advocacy. Among the things that are reclaimed here are images of God, the self-understanding of religious communities, and key religious ideas and concepts such as notions of sin and salvation across the religious traditions. If sin is no longer merely a private matter but a matter of broader relationships that include workers, employers, and God, salvation is no longer merely a private matter either but has to do with the restoration of these relationships.[11]

In the encounters of religion and labor, the idea of religion itself changes, as religion can no longer be conceived of as merely a private or an otherworldly matter. Religion, informed by matters of work and labor, can inspire politics, economics, and everyday life in progressive fashion without having to dictate the outcomes. Theological work and education are an inextricable part of these processes as well.

As religion is reshaped in the tensions of life that affect working people, it can reclaim its roles as an ally and an agent in the struggle for the common good. Without being reshaped in these ways, religion may well support a social project here and there, as often happens, but it will not be able to make much of a difference. This is what is currently happening in many places: religious communities are becoming more active outside of their buildings and beyond their membership, but this engagement is rarely allowed to impact their faith and their worship. Consequently, there is often a split between those members who are active in the world and who have become disillusioned with faith and worship and those members who uphold faith and worship in whatever form they might take at the moment but who see little need for engagement of the world. These splits can be observed even in the world of higher religious education and the seminaries.

Unfortunately, many communities of faith in the United States practice status quo forms of religion, even when they make efforts to help the poor and the needy. This is true even when they offer some mild critiques of the system. This happens, for instance, when these communities act in terms of patronizing images of God (whether they call it charity or advocacy) and thus fail to respect the agency of the people. As a result, a good deal of faith-based organizing leads us right back into the hands of the system. Without attention to the deeper theological issues, religion will more likely remain part of the problem rather than the solution.

Even when their practice is more solid, one of my experiences of working with faith-based community organizers and their communities and churches is that many are hesitant to ask the deeper theological questions implied by their practice. They have internalized a situation in which people who support the poor are called saints and people who ask why they are poor are called socialists, communists, or simply leftists (paraphrasing Dom Hélder Câmara).

In this cultural climate, the Occupy Wall Street movement was significant because it dared to raise such questions ("Why are so many people poor?" "Why are the 99 percent no longer getting ahead?") again for our time, tied to the realities of class and the tensions between the classes (class struggle) that have been hidden for so long.[12] These questions allow for deeper theological questions to be raised: Where is God in this situation? What is Jesus doing? And what does it really mean to be a religious community that is not self-centered?

The latter question, in particular, raises questions of religious communities from the inside that we have not heard spelled out so clearly in a long time, despite Joerg spending the past three decades involved in seminary education. As Frederick Herzog, one of the forgotten original liberation theologians in the United States, used to say in relation to the Christian church, we need to stop idealizing about it and start analyzing it instead.[13] Other religious communities might learn from this attitude as well. Without a clear analysis of religious communities and how they are part of the problem, rallying the church in support of labor is bound to fail because matters remain at the surface.

Labor can help us sort out two of the most burning issues that confront us today and that are closely connected: capitalism and religion. Christianity has a special place in this situation because it is religion that has perhaps been most closely connected with the development of capitalism and that has shored up some of its key developments.[14] This is one reason we pay special attention to Christianity, in addition to the fact that it is the most widely practiced religion by working people in the United States. At the same time, it is also becoming clear that Christianity has important resources that help us provide alternatives.

Unfortunately, religion in general and Christianity in particular is often unaware of the role it plays in matters of labor and economics. Much of the support it gives to the status quo happens unconsciously. By spiritualizing religion, for instance, it withdraws from the world but endorses it by doing so—when Sunday or other religious holidays are considered separate from the rest of the week, the dominant powers are free to do as they please. Furthermore, by envisioning God in terms of the dominant powers—another move that often happens unconsciously—religion provides a justification for the status quo without ever noticing what is going on.

Moralizing religion often does not fare much better than spiritualizing it. While there are some exceptions, religion often endorses the morals of the status quo, assuming that those are the genuine morals of religion. Yet many values endorsed by conservative Christians, for instance, are not much older than a couple of decades and have little to do with the values of the Bible. The idea that women should limit themselves to taking care of the private realm, staying at home, cooking, cleaning, and providing child care goes back not much further than the nineteenth century. Throughout history, women have contributed to work outside the house, in the community and in the fields. Moreover, not long ago conservative religious morality in the United States allowed for slavery, assuming it was God's will. And whatever conclusions people of faith may draw about sexuality, those who condemn homosexual relations altogether often overlook that nowhere in the Bible is there a prohibition of committed monogamous relationships between people of the same sex.

Worst of all, much of religion today is unclear about its purpose. As a result, religion has become equated with a focus on otherworldly reality or with some form of morality tied to maintain the conventions of the recent past—which is what the words spirituality and morality mean to many—and is thus relegated to a sphere of life that is only of concern to people with special interests in otherworldly things or in narrow expressions of morality.

The good news is that the encounter with labor can help religion find its purpose again. The Abrahamic spiritualities or moralities that are emerging in this encounter are not vague, and neither are they primarily otherworldly or narrow. Spirituality here describes a way of life that values human work, productivity, and creativity, with a focus on that which benefits the world as a whole, both human communities and nonhuman communities. This purpose is not narrowly conceived, but it allows us to draw some lines between ways of life that are beneficial and ways of life that are not.

This leads us to a final point where religion needs help. Because of a widespread lack of purpose, people of faith often lack an understanding of limits and borders. The only distinction they are able make is between people of faith and people who reject faith, or between theists and atheists. But this is by no means the most interesting distinction, considering that the tensions of work in the United States are usually between employers who are religious and workers who are religious as well. The class struggle is not waged between people of faith and people who reject faith; it is waged against working people who are usually members of religious communities by corporations whose CEOs are likely to be members of religious communities as well and whose board meetings begin with a prayer.

The most interesting theological question is not whether people believe in God or not, but in what gods they believe or refuse to believe. The Romans had good reasons to consider the early Christians atheists, because they refused to believe in the gods of the dominant status quo.

For the most part, religion has no clue what to do with these tensions, or with tensions in general. In fact, most people of faith refuse to acknowledge tensions within their families and communities, which is why sexual abuse often goes unreported, racism is not challenged, and economic exploitation is overlooked. The result is that in all of these situations, those who represent the dominant powers win out. And because the depth of the tensions is not acknowledged, calls to reconciliation and love are not only shallow but likely perpetuate the problem.

In these cases, labor presents another challenge to religion that is not foreign to many of our traditions: What would it mean to side with those who are oppressed and exploited rather than to stay neutral in situations of injustice? What would it mean to confront sin and evil rather than to accommodate to the status quo? Organizers know that they need a target. What if religion could help us with that? With the support of religion, it may be possible to identify targets without demonizing individuals, according to the old saying "Hate the sin, love the sinner?"

In sum, traditional religious notions such as sin and salvation, or conversion and repentance, do not have to be abandoned. Just the opposite: in the struggle against injustice they come to life again and make a decisive difference. Even the fire-and-brimstone sermons of yesterday have not lost any of their relevance, although their target is now different. Instead of proclaiming judgment against the masses of working people, judgment is proclaimed against a sinful situation—the absolute maximization of profit at all cost— that is harming humanity and the globe in unprecedented ways. The goal is not feeling guilty but instead repentance and conversion, which in the Hebrew traditions was always a practical thing: turning around and going the other way.[15]

The Future of Religion

Religion ebbs and flows. In the United States, religion has enjoyed great success for many years. Today, however, religion has run into some troubles. Interest in organized religion is waning, particularly in the mainline churches of Christianity. In their efforts to stem the tide, church officials are often trying to reproduce past successes. This happens by reminiscing about better times, dressing up old forms and contents in new garbs, and trying to accommodate to what is perceived as the majority opinion.

Some of this might work, were it not for the fact that the public image of religion in the United States is tied to a religious landslide that was engineered by the Religious Right with the support of corporate America.[16] For some decades now, the Religious Right managed to present itself as more faithful and orthodox, more concerned about traditional values, and it created the impression that it was closer to the origins of Christianity because it was referencing the past. This method, to be sure, betrayed a false logic: upholding the family values of the 1950s does not necessarily mean returning to the values of Jesus. The 1950s-values are not necessarily closer to the values of Jesus than the values of the twenty-first century; being older does not necessarily mean truer to the origins.

A recent study by the Brookings Institution provides another framework for the future of religion:

> The religious right spoke to the country's worries about social change. The religious progressive movement speaks to the country's desire for

economic change. In the late 20th century, "family values" were invoked in opposition to what many saw (and feared) as a cultural revolution. In the early 21st century, family stability is most threatened by an economic revolution that has created a growing gap between the economy's productivity gains and the wage growth of most American workers.[17]

While the supporters of the religious right may not find themselves hitting rock bottom anytime soon, in this chapter we are interested in the future of the other kind of religion.

As the report of the Brookings Institution notes, the concern of economic justice may prove to be the fertile ground of this era.[18] As people are concerned about increasing inequalities and injustices, particularly in the world of work and labor where it affects them the most, they are also paying attention to how these things play out in the church. And things do not look good. Forty-five percent of those who had been raised evangelical, 43 percent of those raised Catholic, and 31 percent of those raised in a mainline Protestant denomination said the focus on "money and power" was an important reason they no longer associated with a church.[19]

In other words, by accommodating to the interests of the dominant powers, religion has gained some prestige, but it has also lost a great deal, if not everything. More and more people are getting tired of religion playing the wingman of the status quo. And, what is perhaps most important of all, those now getting tired of dominant religion might be the ones who actually care more about religion than those who continue to go through the motions without asking questions. If religion keeps losing those who care, it doesn't have much of a future.

When religion gets involved in the tensions of real life, things change. Here is where the struggles of work and of labor can help. Far from being just one more outlet for socially engaged people of faith, engaging in the struggles of work and of labor can help us reclaim the heart of our various religions. If God has gone before us in these struggles, as many of our religious traditions insist, we will only find God if we look for God there, beyond where we currently are. This insight was powerfully expressed by a German theologian who fought the false religion of German fascism, Dietrich Bonhoeffer.[20]

While the future of religion will depend on how we deal with these issues, religion in the past has also been decided along these lines. How has religion been able to maintain an edge in the midst of thousands of temptations to assimilate to the status quo through the millennia? We would argue that it is joining the people and the divine in the grassroots struggles that has kept religion alive.[21] Religion has been deeply shaped, for instance, through the efforts of a St. Francis to reconnect the church with the poor of the early centuries, through taking a stand in the peasant wars of early modernity that informed some of the Protestant reformers like Thomas Müntzer, and through the experiences of the African slaves in the United States, shaping both Christianity and ultimately even Islam.[22] These movements have been so powerful that we still use some of their traditions in worship today, even though much of it has been domesticated.

Contrary to what mainline religion wants us to believe, the close relationship between labor and religion is not a new idea. In the creation stories, God works and rests, Moses is involved in labor issues, and so are Jesus and Muhammad. Slightly over a century ago, many of the churches in the United States had the good sense to support the concerns of working people. Ending child labor, instituting the eight-hour workday and the weekend, and fighting for respect for women at work were causes supported by many people of faith.

Unlike today, even collective bargaining (negotiations between employers and organized employees) was actively supported by many of the mainline churches in late nineteenth and early twentieth century.[23] Today, the official documents of many mainline denominations still support collective bargaining, but only a small percentage of members is even aware of this, and even fewer support this matter at a time when collective bargaining is under severe attack.[24] Who could deny that religion learned a great deal in these efforts to support labor? The God worshipped by these religions must have looked different than the God of capitalism, whose main goal is the maximization of profit, which—according to popular belief—is supposed to help everyone.

One example for how the connection with issues of work and labor can help shape the future of religion comes from an experience on the ground. After we gave a presentation on religion and labor to a group of Latino construction workers, many expressed their concern that religion was more a problem than a help. They pointed out that their employers were people of faith as well and that this made little difference at work. Moreover, they argued, faith might actually be harmful to workers if it made them more docile and submissive at work. To these construction workers, the conventional religious values they connected with religion, like humility, service, and love of neighbor, only made things worse for working people. In an earlier session, this same group was quite cynical about efforts to change laws in support of workers; they had little hope that this would help, as the power to implement them seemed to be missing.

Another way of understanding religion, however, caught their attention. What if religion were not primarily about ideas and conventional values or about the sort of things that people do when they are off work? What if religion were about struggling communities, real solidarity, the formation of alternative power, and the fight for a new way of life for everyone who works for a living? In these examples religion would not rest on pious ideas but on people bonding together with the divine to make use of their abilities (including their disabilities, to be sure) for the common good.

The future of religion, it seems to us, will depend heavily on whether it manages to develop an edge or whether it continues to accommodate to the status quo. Today this edge shapes up nowhere more clearly than in the relation of religion and labor, and the pushback that those of us engaged in religion and labor are experiencing appears to prove that we are on to something. Accommodating religion rarely experiences pushback.

One example of such an edge may illustrate what we mean. It has been our experience over the years that while the media in Dallas do not like to report on labor issues, they like to report progressive religious stances even less. One situation was particularly memorable, when a TV reporter interviewed Joerg in front of the camera after a protest outside of a Walmart store. As Joerg was wearing a clerical stole, the reporter asked him several questions about why people of faith were supporting these workers. At the end of the interview, Joerg answered one short question about what the grievances of the workers were, repeating what others had said as well. What was aired on TV that night was only his response to that latter question. No mention of religion was made; it seemed we had been censored. Why? We can only surmise, because we hit a nerve.

Labor indeed has the potential to bring out the edge of religion. After a seminar on religion and labor with the statewide Texas AFL-CIO during which we stressed the importance of labor for religion, a young organizer stood up in the back of the room and asked whether we were suggesting that labor should begin to lobby religion, just like it was lobbying politics. A better way to phrase this concern might be to talk about organizing religion: people of faith—many of whom are working people—can pull together and organize so that religion can reclaim its edge. How else are we going to prevent the dominant powers of this world from shaping religion in their image?

The future of religion does not primarily lie in the hands of professionals. Religious leaders are often conditioned—by training or survival instincts—to serve the interests of power and money. The future of religion lies in the hands of people of faith who need to organize in order to make a difference. When this happens, the horizons of the leaders broaden and some of them take heart and gain courage.[25]

Such organizing can happen in different ways; working people reading the Bible together in light of their everyday struggles is part of it, as is praying and practicing their faith together in the real world. Organizing religious communities can also mean that working people pool their donations in order to address the real needs of the community, thus providing alternatives to the interests of the larger donors who frequently shape the direction of religious communities and the interests of the religious leadership.

Radicalizing Interfaith and Interreligious Dialogues

Several interfaith groups have been supportive of the concerns of working people. Organizations like Interfaith Worker Justice (IWJ), based in Chicago, and Clergy and Laity United for Economic Justice (CLUE) in various locations in California have successfully mobilized and organized members from various religious groups, including Jews, Muslims, Christians, Buddhists, Sikhs, and others.[26]

When members of various religions work together, the likelihood that a campaign is successful increases. Moreover, since it is unusual in our society for people of different faiths to collaborate, the public often takes greater notice. Bringing clergy and officials of various religions to events further highlights interreligious efforts, especially when they wear vestments and present other symbols of their faith traditions.

Nevertheless, the value of these interfaith collaborations is even greater when deep solidarity among the various religions is established. Understanding that we are facing similar problems and working together to overcome them is a powerful bond that allows us to use our differences constructively and to value them in new ways. In other words, not only does labor win when religions work together, religions themselves gain as well.

Deep solidarity, as mentioned earlier, does not eradicate differences but puts them to work for the common good. When the various religions come together in the support of working people, they can bring to bear the particular strengths of their traditions without the need to claim that we are all alike. The Jewish concern for the well-being of the community, the Christian understanding of God embodied in Jesus the construction worker, and the strong sense of God's justice in Muslim traditions all make important contributions. The same is true for the Buddhist emphasis on compassion, a vital religious tradition that is beyond the purview of this book. These differences empower the movement, each in their own ways. Recognizing this diversity helps expand our bases, and it will make the representatives of various religions more interested in learning from each other.

Organizers might feel they are doing religion and the labor movement a favor when they point out the similarities of the various religions. Yet declaring that all religions are basically saying the same thing is counterproductive for various reasons. First of all, such declarations often show a lack of respect for the different religions and their worlds. Those who have studied their own religion and other religions for a long time are much more careful when it comes to claiming the same essence of all religions.[27] Second, assuming that all religions are the same means to lose the wealth of the different insights and strengths that different religions can bring to the struggle. Finally, stating that religions are the same precludes the possibility that religions can and need to learn from each other.

Only after an initial appreciation for the differences between the various religions does it make sense to reflect on the similarities that lead us to collaborate. In the common struggle we begin to compare notes on what our religious traditions might have to contribute and where the convergences are. What if Moses, Jesus, Muhammad, and Buddha, were not just great religious leaders but also the leaders of movements that struggled for the common good? What if our traditional notions of love and justice share a common resistance to capitalist notions of "love" and "justice" (we will come back to this in the next chapter)? What emerges here is not just a new way of collaborating in deep solidarity but a whole new model of interreligious and interfaith dialogue.[28]

The result of these interfaith and interreligious encounters is a closer relationship between the various faiths that allows for deeper appreciation and respect. This does not mean that all lines of separation should disappear. Lines of distinction and separation are still drawn, but differently. While a Christian and a Muslim who collaborate on matters of work discover their unity in difference, they also discover what separates them from certain members of their own faith traditions. Christians might find that there is a line of separation between those Christians who see God supporting working people and those who see God supporting the dominant powers in the corporations. And Muslims might find that there is a deeper gap between Muslims who have to work for a living and Muslims who are controlling the wealth of their communities.[29]

Where the lines are drawn makes all the difference. Playing off the various religions against each other, like telling Christians that Muslims are out to get them or telling Muslims that Christians are trying to water down their values is not a harmless reflection on culture. This widespread assumption of a clash between cultures or religions is deeply troublesome because it serves as a cover up for the global struggle that is waged against working people of all religions.[30] When working people of faith understand where the lines are drawn for them, they can begin redrawing the lines not only between the religions but also between the religions and social movements.

Working people of faith who support other working people may find themselves in closer proximity with the Occupy Wall Street movement, for instance, than they ever imagined.[31] To use an expression by Columbia professor Hamid Dabashi, our religious traditions need to become religions-in-the-world rather than claiming the abstract idea of world religions.[32]

When deep solidarity includes deep religious solidarity, new things are destined to happen. And the old divide and conquer tactics cease to split the movement because we know we share common interests that go deep and have developed a trust that weathers the storms of daily efforts of coalition building. Religion can indeed learn a great deal from labor.

Religion Radicalizing Labor

Beyond the Cheap Date

Just as religion appears to be at its best when it is located in the communal struggles of everyday life, concerns for work and labor are at their best when put in relation to the deepest hopes and aspirations of people and their communities. This insight is embodied in many religious traditions that have been shaped by working people.

Unfortunately, just like a lot of religious people do not know what their religion is about, working people who are members of unions are often not quite clear what their organizations stand for either. Narrow or distorted views are common in both cases. How many people of faith and how many union members assume that their organizations are mainly about two things: paying dues and getting some clearly defined services in return? And how many are measuring the value of their organizations and their membership in terms of how dues and services measure up?

These confusions are not mere accidents. In the case of labor unions, one argument often used by their opponents is that the dues benefit "union bosses" rather than the members, based on the idea that dues and services (narrow conceptions of short-term personal gain) are all that matters. In the case of religious communities, there is fierce competition that suggests people of faith should join those groups that give them the most benefits for their dues—be it a fun place for their children, the promised profits of the gospel of prosperity, or the networking opportunities for business people in mainline faith communities. What is too often missing is an understanding that both religious communities and labor unions are designed to serve the broader common good.

Just as labor helped us rediscover the edge of religion, we believe that religion can help us rediscover and reclaim the edge of labor. This is not merely a matter of revitalizing labor unions, just like we are not merely concerned with revitalizing existing religious communities. What we are interested in is reclaiming the significance, the energy, and the power of labor, just like we are interested in reclaiming the significance, the energy, and the power of religion. Together, religion and labor can change the world.

None of this can happen when religion is treated like a cheap date for labor or community organizing, as has sometimes been the case. Religion is not merely the place where organizers can mobilize some warm bodies or "rent a collar," as the saying goes; religion is more important than that. Religious traditions, as we will demonstrate, can provide important resources that help us clarify the importance of work and labor. Likewise, religions provide a sort of critical thinking that can be useful: asking questions about what really matters in life, religions can help us question the dominant powers of our age and identify alternative powers.

Take the example of production, which is a key factor of mainline economic thinking that follows simple rules of supply and demand, leading to the accumulation of profit. While production seems to be a noncontroversial issue in economics, the perspective of production changes dramatically when viewed from the perspective of labor: work matters not just in terms of profit but in terms of the actual contributions that working people make to the community, shaping history from the bottom up, as it were. Here we find a parallel to various ancient Abrahamic traditions that address matters of labor. These traditions, which are quite prominent in the biblical texts, have often been neglected in the history of religion, reminding us of the extent to which religious concerns are shaped by the economic status quo.

Nevertheless, that Moses (recognized in Judaism, Christianity, and Islam) organized laboring slaves and that Jesus was a construction worker, as pointed out above, may turn out to be more important than anyone might have expected. People of faith should ask themselves why God did not choose to manifest divine power at the top levels of ancient empires like Egypt, or why God did not become human in an upper-class Jewish family. Would this not have had all sorts of advantages for the promotion of religion, "all other things being equal," as the economists say? Apparently, all other things are not equal in these cases. God's relation to production and labor appears to be significant and changes our perspectives.

One important theological implication of God's social location in the world of labor is that Moses, Amos, David (a shepherd before he became king), Jesus, Peter, Paul, Mary, Muhammad (who also started out as a shepherd, as did many of the other prophets in Islam[1]), and other religious leaders shared the perspective of working people. As a result, they were able to see more clearly what the real problems were, but they were also able to see what difference working people can make in the world.

Equally important, from the perspective of work and labor they were able to gain fresh visions of God, cutting through the many images of false gods, which enslaved people—from the slaves in Egypt in the case of Moses, to the peasants at the margins of the Roman Empire in the case of Jesus and the disciples. Moreover, it seems that by being in touch with the needs of the people, desire was created for resistance as God appeared in unexpected and life-changing ways.

Abrahamic Perspectives on Labor

The goal of this chapter is to introduce the broader perspective that the labor movement needs, including a longer view of history and alternative power, and to give reasons for why we can be cautiously hopeful. Religion, and the Abrahamic traditions in particular, provides this broader perspective, as many religions that are practiced today took shape in the struggles with various empires at various times. Alternative power prevailed as the various empires of history collapsed (Egypt, Babylonia, Rome, Spain, etc.). In other words, labor can learn a few things from religion, especially in the United States, which remains the most religious of the Western industrialized countries. Failing to address religion does not mean it will go away; it means that religion will be used in service to the dominant powers and the corporations, as it often is.[2]

In many of the Abrahamic religious traditions, the view from the perspective of working people is indispensable. This means that the concerns of working people and of labor are not just social concerns for some who happen to care about this particular issue; these concerns are at the heart of these religious traditions themselves. Without paying attention to the concerns of work and labor these religions, including their images of God, are easily misunderstood and distorted.

For example, the legacy of Moses, shared by Judaism, Christianity, and Islam cannot be conceived without his solidarity with the Hebrew slaves in Egypt. The liberation from Egypt is not just the backdrop of a harmless religious story; it is at the heart of the Abrahamic traditions. The legacy of Jesus cannot be conceived without his solidarity with working people of his own time. Christianity, when it forgets this fact, is often perverted into something opposing workers. The legacy of Muhammad is likewise tied to a concern for the well-being of the working people of his time, many of whom were being defrauded in the transition from a tribal to a mercantile society where the traders gathered substantial fortunes at the expense of the masses. The concerns of Islam, which are so often misunderstood by outsiders, appear in new light when this is taken into account.

The central celebrations of these three religions demonstrate what we are trying to say here. Passover, Christmas, and Ramadan are closely tied to the concerns of working people and of labor. Unfortunately, this is not yet fully recognized, even by those who have made efforts to bring together concerns of religion and labor. Yet take a closer look at the deeper meanings of these celebrations.

Judaism's celebration of the Passover is an annual reminder of the liberation from slavery in Egypt. Few other religious rituals are as strongly grounded in an act of liberation. This liberation, as should be immediately clear, was not merely a spiritual matter; rather, liberation affects everything, including economics, politics, community, personal relationships, and even the most intimate relationships people had.

The Passover celebration is an act of remembering the slavery in Egypt and liberation from it. It begins with the Passover Seder, a ritual meal during which the Passover story is retold. The children present at the table are encouraged to join in the conversation about the Exodus and to raise questions about the story. The first question the children are encouraged to ask is, "Why is this night different from all other nights?"

One of the key elements of the Passover Seder is unleavened bread—a reminder that the Israelites left in such a hurry that they had no time to wait for the dough to rise. Another element is the Maror, bitter herbs (Exodus 12:8), as a reminder of the bitterness of slavery. On the last day of Passover (after seven or eight days), the passing through the Red Sea is celebrated, commemorating both the miraculous rescue and the drowning of the Egyptian army.

If religion is understood in terms of people's daily lives, it is not hard to see the many connections of this struggle to the struggle of working people today. Oppression and exploitation are still real-life experiences, as are stories of liberation. These connections are made explicit today in the so-called "Labor Seders," organized by the Jewish Labor Committee since the year 2000.[3] The focus is on remembering that the struggle for liberation is ongoing. The following parallels between the ancient times and today are highlighted: persecution, oppressive taskmasters, impossible work demands, work quotas, and finally, a struggle for freedom.[4]

One of the Christian celebrations most deeply connected with work and labor is Christmas. Rather than the celebration of consumption—as capitalism has perverted its meaning—Christians celebrate the birth of the Christ, the son of God, acknowledged by most traditions as both human and divine. God chose to become a human construction worker, most likely a day laborer who would have known the hardships of work firsthand. This arrangement was certainly not the easiest or most advantageous for the spread of the message, and so it appears to be more than a historical accident or a mistake. Moreover, what good was a birth in the precarious situation of a barn supposed to do? Why make a spectacular announcement of this birth to lower working-class shepherds—sending the heavenly choir of angels no less—rather than the upper crust of the country (Luke 2:7–10)?

What Christians celebrate at Christmas is not merely that God became human, but that God became a lowly worker who practiced "deep solidarity" with ordinary working people from the beginning to the end of his life. And this was a solidarity that contributed to his death on a cross of the Roman Empire. There is a deeper significance to "God as worker" at the core of the Christian faith, and who better to explore what this means than working people, both past and present?

Keep in mind that the symbols of Christmas, like shepherds and sheep for instance, are not simply cute, romantic adornments of a mystical event. They are reminders of God's unflinching solidarity with working people. Even the angels join in deep solidarity with working people as they announce this birth to shepherds rather than large landowners or political and religious leaders. We are not aware of any efforts to celebrate a "Labor Christmas," like some of the Jewish faithful celebrate a Labor Seder, but it would be completely appropriate. The common critiques of consumerism leveled around Christmastime would sound very different and be directed at different targets: rather than blaming consumers, people might focus on those with an interest in fueling consumerism and how working people are exploited to maintain the existing power structure. The mythical elves of Santa might also be seen in a different light, joining the ranks of exploited workers.[5]

In Islam, the month of Ramadan mandates fasting, one of the five pillars of Islam. Ramadan is the commemoration of the first revelation of the Qur'an given to the prophet Muhammad. All other sacred scriptures, including the Torah, the Psalms, and the Gospels are believed to have been revealed during Ramadan as well. Fasting is observed for 29 or 30 days in a row, from dawn to sunset.

Ramadan is a time of increased self-discipline, prayer, and charity (the latter two are also among the five pillars of Islam). One interpretation of fasting during Ramadan is that this helps the faithful to know what it might feel like to be poor and to be in solidarity with the poor. Empathy and support for the poor is not just an ethical commandment in Islam—it is tied to the heart of faith because it reflects the will of God. In Indonesia, the country with the world's largest Muslim population, employees receive a one-month bonus after the end of Ramadan, comparable to Christmas bonuses. Muslims continue to work during Ramadan, as balance between worship and work is encouraged by the Prophet. In some countries, labor law stipulates that working hours are reduced to six hours per day during Ramadan.

Like the Christian celebrations of Christmas, some Muslims have pointed out that Ramadan has also been perverted by capitalism. Yet perversion never has the final word. Muslim scholar Tariq Ramadan, for instance, argues that the celebration of Ramadan could inspire resistance to the capitalist ethos of limitless growth and the infinite accumulation of profits. He suggests that the celebration of Ramadan might help us conceive of qualitative improvement of people's lives rather than purely quantitative growth.[6]

These three major religious celebrations are important, however, not merely for the profound message each conveys in support of working people, but also because of the community created around them. As Christian ethicist Melissa Snarr has pointed out, ritual helps form collective identity, because it is a *"low-risk* form of activism." Such ritual also challenges the separation of the sacred and the world, teaching us that labor is not merely a worldly issue but also a sacred concern and a way of embodying the sacred.[7] Each of these observations is important: for the most part, traditional religious rituals are indeed low-risk, providing safe means of communal self-expression.[8] Celebrating Passover, Christmas, or Ramadan provides a safe space for exploring alternative ways of life both in the imagination and in practice.

Moreover, the rituals of Passover, Christmas, and Ramadan are all places where religion becomes public, pushing beyond narrow boundaries of what is considered the sacred: the liberation of the Exodus, the birth of Jesus as worker, and the practice of fasting during Ramadan all have implications not just for religious practice but for the transformation of the world. In each case, the message is not just addressing the mind. The heart and the body are addressed as well—religion is not just a matter of deep thinking but also of deep feeling and of deep embodiment. Finally, the celebrations of Passover, Christmas, and Ramadan teach important lessons about God's presence that are often forgotten or repressed. In each case, God is at work in places where the dominant system least expects it: in acts of liberation from enslavement (Passover), acts of solidarity with working people (Christmas), and acts of resistance to limitless profit (Ramadan).

Justice

Justice is one of the key theological terms in the Abrahamic religions, even though this is often overlooked. Even working people seem to identify religion with charity rather than justice.[9] In Judaism, the notion of justice is tied to the covenants with God. In Christianity, justice is one of the key concerns of the New Testament, not only in Jesus' message but also in Paul's. In Islam, it has been argued that justice is the most fundamental value, as Allah in the Qur'an is called *'Adil*, "just."[10]

Justice in the Abrahamic traditions is in direct contrast to what justice means in capitalist societies, where justice is often applied as a formal principle. According to capitalist economist Friedrich von Hayek, justice means "the fair and impartial application of legal, moral and perhaps customary rules."[11] Capitalism considers all participants in the market to be equal. This is not the case, of course, in the real world. There is a substantial difference between large and small participants in the market. The largest corporations have a significantly stronger position than smaller corporations or even workers. The so-called free trade agreements, like the North American Free Trade Agreement (NAFTA) and the Trans Pacific Partnership (TPP), seek to boost free markets, even though they contain many stipulations intended to boost the position of the more powerful players in the market.[12]

Yet significant problems remain even if market relations were fair and balanced and no special deals were made that give preferential treatment to the more powerful participants in the market. When unequals are made to compete on level ground, the outcome can easily be predicted. A five-year-old child, for example, intuitively understands why a race where the same rules apply to a five-year-old and an eleven-year-old cannot be considered to be fair or just; treating a five-year-old and an eleven-year-old exactly alike in a competitive situation would indeed be unjust. The equal treatment of unequals may well be the greatest injustice of all, especially in situations of severe power differentials, the kind that we find in the relationship of employers and employees of large corporations.[13]

Based on this simple insight it is not hard to see why an economy, in which significant differentials of power and wealth exist, cannot lead to greater justice for all. When working people have nothing to sell but their labor, and when they have little other support from the community or the law, the corporations who employ them have a tremendous advantage. This advantage is compounded under the conditions of globalization, when workers are being played off against each other on the global scene. The practice of union busting, designed to take away any remaining power that workers might have in the name of fairness, further adds to the lop-sided situation.

Justice defined as fairness is, therefore, not a helpful concept for working people because it is unable to deal with situations of grave power differentials, which we experience every day. Alternative perspectives on justice emerge from those who are the losers in the current situation, like workers, small business owners, and the growing masses of those who cannot find or keep a job in an economy where jobs are increasingly under pressure. Here, the Abrahamic religious traditions can make significant contributions, as many of their traditions derive from the perspective of people under pressure and because they find the divine there.

God, in these traditions, is not neutral like Lady Justice, the Roman goddess who is traditionally portrayed with a blindfold, and a pair of scales and a sword in each hand. Divine neutrality amounts not to justice but to injustice. As Farid Esack, a South African Muslim liberation theologian has pointed out, according to the Qur'an, neutrality or objectivity in the context of oppression is a sin.[14]

In the Jewish traditions, on which the Christian and Islamic traditions are building, justice means not being neutral but being in solidarity with those who experience injustice and taking the sides of those who have been marginalized and excluded from the community. In many texts of the Hebrew Bible, for instance, justice refers not to the notion of fairness but to a covenant, that is, to a relationship between God and humanity that is initiated by God. This relationship is expressed in terms of God's faithfulness, which implies God's special concern for those pushed to the margins of the covenant and for those who are excluded by some who are under the mistaken impression that their way of life is favored by God.[15]

In the New Testament, Jesus often takes the sides of the oppressed over and against the oppressors (see, for instance, his biting critique of dominant groups like the Pharisees in Matt. 23:1–36). In Islam, the Qur'an expresses a similar concern when it gives the following advice: "And if two factions among the believers should fight, then make settlement between the two. But if one of them oppresses the other, then fight against the one that oppresses until it returns to the ordinance of Allah (49:9)."[16] In sum, Judaism, Christianity, and Islam all share a special concern for the oppressed, often put in terms of helping the widows, the orphans, the strangers, and the poor.

What the Abrahamic notions of justice have in common is their focus on community and solidarity, the latter a term that resonates with the labor movement and puts it on a strong religious foundation. The Hebrew verb *sdq* means to be faithful to the community that was established by the covenant with God.[17] The Greek term *dikaiosyné*, as used in the New Testament, also reflects this emphasis on communal relationship. Although there is no uniform notion of justice in the New Testament, justice tends to include both the relations between human beings and the relation to God.[18] In Islam, likewise, justice (the Arab terms for justice, *quist* and *'adl*, used interchangeably in the Qur'an[19]) is defined in relation to the divine (as a witness to Allah) and has implications for how people treat each other (Qur'an 4:135). As Jewish scholar Aryeh Cohen points out from a Rabbinic Jewish perspective, the problem is the unequal relationship between worker and employer, which is never merely a private matter since the community has an interest in it as well.[20] Keep in mind that these relationships are never just a matter of money or of economics but of life as a whole.

In the writings of the prophets of the Hebrew Bible, the term *justice* addresses specifically the distorted relationships between the rich and the poor, caused by oppressive actions of the rich, who "trample on the poor" (Amos 5:11), an action that also distorts the relationship with God.[21] This distortion of relationships by oppression is a concern in various parts of the Hebrew Bible—the Psalms come to mind as another prominent example.[22] It can also be found in Jesus's sayings as reported both in the Christian New Testament and in the Qur'an, where Jesus is honored as a prophet. Justice in all these cases aims at ending oppression by challenging the oppressors, with the goal of restoring broken relationships with others and with God.

The primary concern of justice is, thus, not so much helping those in need but overcoming oppressive relationships and learning how to create more genuine relationships and what we are calling deep solidarity, both with other human beings and with God. The apostle Paul's notion of justification can be seen in a similar light: not simply as a religious transaction but as a manifestation of God's justice in the midst of the massive injustices of the Roman Empire. Justification, in Paul's use of the term, resists the injustices of the powerful who boast in their own power (Eph. 2:9) and reconstructs distorted relationships.[23]

As a result, justice, as restoring broken relationships, needs to address the power differentials between oppressors and oppressed, and it is partisan insofar as God sides with those who are trampled underfoot. Peruvian Christian liberation theologian Gustavo Gutiérrez's reflections match our reflections of this point: "To deal with a poor man or woman as Yahweh dealt with his people—this is what it is to be just." And: "To be just is to be faithful to the covenant. . . . Justice in the Bible is what unites one's relationship with the poor to one's relationship with God."[24]

The image of the divine emerging here is dynamic. A God who opts for those whose relationships have been violated can never be pinned down in terms of an abstract notion of fairness. People of faith sometimes get sidetracked wondering if we are talking about "spiritual" or "social" processes here; is this a matter of "social justice" or some other sort of justice? This question is moot, as the Abrahamic traditions do not operate with this division: there is only one justice. If God is God of all things—not just of the private sphere and of privatized religion—there is no way to separate those realms.

Justice in the Abrahamic traditions has to do, therefore, with a particular concern for the restoration of relationships with those who are being pushed to the margins of the covenant, such as the proverbial widows, orphans, strangers, and the poor of the Hebrew Bible and the Qur'an, and the fishermen, prostitutes, tax collectors, and the poor and sick of the New Testament. In this context, restoration of relationship with the oppressed is not simply a social issue or the moral consequence of faith; rather, the quality of faith itself, and the relationship with the divine is closely connected to the restoration of relationships among the people. Distortions in relations to others get reproduced in distortions in relations to God, and vice versa.[25]

These insights are helpful in various ways. First, rather than talk about justice in terms of a grand idea, we need to begin to organize our movements from particular experiences of injustice and power. Who wins and who loses? What would it take to turn things around? Notions of fairness and balance are unlikely to be strong enough to resist injustice that has become institutionalized.

Second, injustice in our case has to do specifically with the dramatic differences in the valuation of productivity. Why should working people, both blue and white collar, make hundreds of times less than upper-level managers? Why are wages cut when workers are becoming more productive all the time? Justice in this case has nothing to do with the giving of alms or with charity for working people. Justice means to value the productivity of workers and to reconstruct the relationships between those who work and those who manage. Religion can help when we observe how even God is productive through work as well. Such alternative takes on productivity are something mainline religion is often unable to produce, because mainliners rarely realize that the divine is actually at work from below rather than from above; for similar reasons, mainline economics misses this alternative take on productivity as well.

Third, justice that deals with the specific injustices of work and labor helps us rethink solidarity in the face of distorted economic relations. Economic pressures tend to weld together people who are vastly different—including those white-collar employees (often white and male) who are now also experiencing the economic squeeze firsthand. This is what we mean by deep solidarity. People of faith could be ahead of the game if they realized that the distortion of economic relations is a central issue in the sacred texts of the Abrahamic traditions, Tanakh, Bible, and Qur'an, once again, not merely as a social or ethical issue, but also in terms of the distortion of our relations to each other and to the divine.

Taking Sides

One of the interesting convergences between the traditions of labor and of the three Abrahamic religions is that they all understand the necessity to take sides in situations of injustice and grave power differentials. This is perhaps the biggest surprise of our argument so far. Taking sides goes against the grain of the common sense of the dominant system, and it goes against the grain of what most well-meaning people might think needs to be done.

Taking sides, however, does not have to mean narrow partisanship or mindless radicalism. Taking sides means to support the well-being of the 99 percent, leaving open the possibility that the 1 percent will see the light and join in this project as well. Some may consider it impossible for a 1 percenter to join the movement, like it is impossible for camel to go through the eye of a needle. But, as Jesus reminded his disciples, nothing is impossible for God (Matt. 19:26). This has been one of the experiences in the Occupy Wall Street movement, where 1 percenters did in fact join the 99 percent.[26]

The labor movement's tradition of taking sides has waxed and waned through the decades. Many working people today, and even some of the unions, believe that it is possible to make everybody happy. Individuals try to please the company and their superiors by working extra hard and overtime, giving up vacation, and never making their voices heard. The results of this approach have been mixed at best, as the fortunes of working people are hardly on the rise. Individuals will never be able to balance the growing inequality of power. Even the representatives of unions, however, have at times forgotten that it is necessary to take sides, assuming that they can find a middle road between workers and their employers. The Abrahamic traditions, as well as the experiences of working people in recent times, remind us that there is no safe middle ground.

In this situation, religion has some unexpected lessons to teach. In the Abrahamic traditions, God is not an entity that keeps out of the struggles of the world. Just the opposite: God engages these struggles and takes the side of the oppressed, challenging the oppressors. Failure to resist oppression and to take sides is, therefore, not just a moral problem—it is also a theological problem. A God who supports the dominant powers at all costs is an idol in these religions. A God whose image is consistent with the image of those among the powerful who remain aloof from the suffering of the world and of the working majority, is not the God of Abraham, Moses, Jesus, and Muhammad.[27]

This insight is expressed in different ways. In Islam, God's Otherness is a central theme.[28] This means that God is not envisioned in terms of human beings. In Judaism and Christianity, on the other hand, God is often portrayed as a worker, although there are also Jewish and Christian traditions where God is seen as different from humanity. The parallels, however, should not be overlooked: in all three religions, God is not easily envisioned in terms of the ruling class. Even when God is called "king," this does not necessarily mean that God is a ruler just like any other monarch or emperor. God as king is often portrayed in opposition to the kings of this world (Psalm 2:1-11).

The Christian tradition is perhaps clearest on this: when it calls Jesus "lord," it is clear from the very beginning that this lord is very different from the Roman emperor, who also bore that title. Jesus as lord is a subversion of all lords. As Christian theologian Karl Barth has observed, God's otherness finds expression in Christ's lowly birth.[29] In other words, divine otherness is not a matter of receding from this world; divine otherness is a matter of taking sides with those who are "othered" by the status quo.

Some of the Jewish and Christian images of God as worker can help us deepen these insights. God is, for instance, envisioned as a craftsman or a metal worker.[30] Other images in the Hebrew Bible portray God as potter. This image challenges not only dominant economic arrangements but also gender stereotypes: in the early history of Israel, pottery was mostly the work of women.[31]

The image of God as garment maker also reflects the work of women in Hebrew times—keep in mind that in ancient times women's work was not narrowly confined to the house. In New Testament times, both men and women worked in textile production.[32] As gardener, God is working with bare hands in the creation story (Genesis 2:8–9), and God is envisioned as farmer, watering plants and sowing. As theologian Robert Banks observes: "There is no hesitation here in identifying God as much with the farm worker as with the farm owner."[33]

Several passages in the Bible talk about God as shepherd. Sheepherding is a common matter in all three Abrahamic religions, and it is usually a marginal and less valued job.[34] Elsewhere, God is spoken of in terms of the profession of a tentmaker—a profession that among the Greek and Roman-educated circles was looked down upon, while in Jewish circles even intellectuals pursued some trade.[35] Finally, God is also envisioned as construction worker and builder.[36]

There is certainly no lack of images in Judaism and Christianity that might help us value work and workers, particularly the kinds of workers that are often discounted and belittled. This has implications for dominant images of God: envisioning God as common worker challenges images of God as absolute king or boss. No easy middle road is possible that would allow us to strike a balance so that God can be seen as both worker and boss at the same time. When God enters into deep solidarity with workers, work is valued in such a way that it cannot easily be devalued again in the search for profit.

In Islam, the need to take the side of the oppressed is equally clear. In Qur'an 4:75, the readers are asked this question: "And what is [the matter] with you that you fight not in the cause of Allah and [for] the oppressed among men, women, and children who say, 'Our Lord, take us out of this city of oppressive people and appoint for us from Yourself a protector and appoint for us from Yourself a helper?'" The divine cause is to take sides in the fight against oppression, and the faithful are expected to be part of it. This fight is not a minor matter. Khali Ur Rehman, chairman of the All Pakistan Federation of Labor, argues that Islam helps us understand that exploitation and usurpation are the causes of all of the world's problems.[37]

In this context, the Islamic notion of jihad can be interpreted in ways that are more faithful to its origins and to our current situation. Contrary to a common misunderstanding in the United States and in Europe, the objective of jihad is not religious supremacy or the formation of an empire; rather, the objective of jihad is the establishment of justice. According to Muslim scholar Farid Esack, jihad means "'to struggle', 'to exert oneself' or to 'spend energy or wealth.'" In the South African liberation struggle, he reports, it meant "striving for truth and justice."[38]

According to Indian Muslim scholar Ali Asghar Engineer, "To engage with unjust social structures and make constant efforts to make life richer and more livable in terms of justice and human dignity is true jihad."[39] Engineer notes that those who practice justice are closer to God. This is the reason, he argues, why historically it was the weaker sections of societies who were attracted to Islam, rather than the privileged and the ruling classes.[40]

In any case, a reversal takes place, which resonates with all three of the Abrahamic traditions. Engineer points out that the the "mustad'ifin," the oppressed, will rule over the earth and inherit it, a theme that is also familiar in Christianity, where the meek shall inherit the earth (Matt.

5:5).[41] The Qur'an 28:5 reads, in reference to the liberation from Egypt: "And We wanted to confer favor upon those who were oppressed in the land and make them leaders and make them inheritors." Jesus' frequent reminders that the last will be the first and the first will be the last (Matt. 20:16, and vice versa in Mark 10:31 and Matt. 19:30) strike a similar note.

The wealthy are not left out of this picture. Wealth that is not used for the common good and the welfare of the community becomes destructive to those who hoard it. The Qur'an (3:180) states: "And let not those who [greedily] withhold what Allah has given them of His bounty ever think that it is better for them. Rather, it is worse for them. Their necks will be encircled by what they withheld on the Day of Resurrection. And to Allah belongs the heritage of the heavens and the earth. And Allah, with what you do, is [fully] Acquainted." Similar concerns can be found in the Jewish and Christian traditions. The prophets of the Hebrew Bible proclaim judgment on the rich who "oppress the poor" and "crush the needy" (Amos 4:1), Jesus blesses the poor but proclaims woe to the rich (Luke 6:24). What if these were all invitations to the wealthy to take sides as well—not with their own kind but with those in need and those who suffer oppression?

There is a wealth of religious texts that make similar statements, and here lies one of the basic lessons for working people and the labor movement, inviting us to explore matters at a deeper level. Taking sides is not primarily a pragmatic matter—taking sides puts us in touch with what is really going on in the world, what "keeps the world together at its core."[42]

Where is God in all of this? Too often dominant religions have claimed God to be on their side in order to shore up their power. One of the lowest points in this history was, no doubt, the witness of the so-called "German Christians" in Nazi Germany. At that time, German Fascism claimed that God was on its side, demonstrated by parading flags into the churches and having clergy and bishops bless the war and the arms used to fight it.

Are working people committing the same mistakes when they claim that God is on their side? History shows that we should not presuppose too quickly that God supports our causes. Nevertheless, not talking about whose side God is on does not solve our problems, as there is always a default position that is endorsed by those who refuse to take sides altogether. In Nazi Germany, for example, many churches tried to stay neutral. It was not until it was all over, however, that they realized they supported the system by not speaking out against it. Today, efforts to stay neutral have similar effects, as the default position locates the divine on the side of the dominant powers. For many people of faith, staying neutral means to consent to leaving God on the side of capitalism and the ongoing maximization of profit. No wonder it appears to many observers—both inside and outside the United States—that American religion has been hijacked by the status quo.

As a result, we need to put our cards on the table. Judaism, Christianity, and Islam envision God supporting working people, particularly when they are under pressure and exploited. Three things ought to be clear: first, God is never on the side of those who refuse to contribute to the common good and who exploit others, no matter how respectable they might appear. Second, God's concern for the community, for the common good, demands that a stand be taken against whatever destroys the community and the common good. Images of God's judgment, common in all three of the Abrahamic religions, are not bad news but good news for the exploited and oppressed. Third, the Abrahamic traditions insist that God is at work in the world, but in places where we least expect it. That God is working alongside working people is significant, even though it does not mean that working people can control God or own God.

Few Americans would suspect that other religions outside of the Abrahamic traditions would have much to say about these matters. Buddhism, for instance, is often caricaturized as the religion of peace. Buddhists, the assumption goes, would rather reconcile differences than take sides in a conflict. Even in conversations with Engaged Buddhists we have at times found a hesitancy to take sides, but in the question of work and labor, neutrality is not an option. No one, not even religious people, can claim that they are not affected by it. The suggestion of a young activist with the Buddhist Peace Fellowship in the San Francisco Bay Area, Kathy Loncke, is worth considering. As she noted, instead of denying the reality of conflict, we might consider engaging in conflict in compassionate ways—"compassionate conflict" was Loncke's expression. Buddhists too are part of the fight for the right cause.[43]

The Future of Labor

At a time when the future of religion is open, the future of the labor movement is open as well. Neither religion nor labor should be limited to particular organizations. If religion is the quest for something that is bigger than us and that we cannot control as individuals, so is labor. Everybody who works for a living is part of labor, even though not everybody realizes this and even though the current legal situation obscures this. The question is: Will people understand and link up with the movements that are already under way? The sky is the limit.

One of the problems that both religion and labor face at present is that their perspectives are still too narrow. Labor and the working people who make up the movement need to examine what the goals are. Is the goal merely stemming the tide that is currently moving against labor; is it a matter of shoring up some status quo that we once enjoyed? Or is the goal elevating more people into the great American middle class that is under pressure as well? Can that be all? Religion, it seems to us, might help us rethink the original goals of labor and working people in more profound ways, without needing to control the outcome.

It may not surprise anybody that unions, just like most religious institutions, are hesitant to critique the broader system from which most of our problems derive. It is much easier to critique clear moral or legal offenses like wage theft, unfair labor practices, or the violations of safety regulations; it is also easier to denounce malpractice in business or wrongdoings common with corporations. The fundamental problem in capitalism, however, is that in the quest for the maximization of profits the corporations are responsible to their stockholders rather than to their workers and that one of the most effective ways to maximize profits is to cut working people's wages, benefits, and to reduce whatever power they might have over themselves and their work.

Labor and religion have the potential to become allies in dealing with these systemic issues, and their futures may depend on how well they do this. We would argue that what is ultimately at stake for religion is whether it is merely a matter of private issues like personal sexuality or the ideas of individuals, or whether it can make contributions to dealing with the life-and-death issues of our time. What is at stake for labor is similar: Are matters of work and labor merely technical issues that can be resolved with contracts and bargaining, or can labor also make contributions to the bigger issues that destroy the lives of billions of people and hurt the planet?[44]

At the same time, labor and religion can become allies in very practical matters. As discussed in the previous chapter, labor can help people of faith understand the importance of organizing. Religious communities will hardly change from the top down. But neither will labor. In what seems to be a surprising turn, studies have found that "religious organizations are three to four times more likely to mobilize a person politically than a union."[45] We are not talking about party politics, of course, but about joining the struggle. One of the advantages of religious communities is that, due to the fact that they are often more homogeneous, working people are able to prove themselves in leadership roles: Construction workers and Walmart workers can practice public speaking, preside over meetings, and negotiate with the pastor. What moves those on the lower rungs of the class structure, according to these studies, however, is not primarily speeches and sermons. What matters is the opportunity to develop civic skills and technique.

It seems to us, however, that two matters belong together here: the development of skills and technique and a deeper awareness of why all of this is important. This awareness is not limited to the mind, it shapes hearts and bodies as well. This is what religion can do, and what it has done throughout the ages. In the United States, neither the abolitionist movement, nor the civil rights movement, and not even the labor movement can be envisioned without the contributions of religion and its abilities to shape people holistically, deep down.[46]

The most important issue of all, however, is the question of power. What power are these movements exercising and what power does religion embody? Too often, both in past history and at present, people assume that there is only one sort of power that will be successful, namely dominant power that operates from the top down. For that reason, some of the leaders in both labor and religion have attempted to wield such dominant power. Some have done so very well and with great success. The problem is, however, that in these cases both labor and religion have been remade in the image of the status quo. Union leaders, clergy, and even images of God were shaped according to the model of powerful CEOs. In these cases, both labor and religion gained power at the expense of the ability to make a real difference and to challenge the dominant system.

As we have seen, many strands of the Abrahamic religious traditions provide us with alternative images of power. In these traditions, the true leaders do not shape up in the image of the "strong man"; rather, leaders shape up in relations of deep solidarity, from within the working majority. This is true even for images of God. The power of the people is a different power than that of the elites, and both labor and religion may have a brighter future if they manage to embrace and pursue this power.

The good news is that some of this is already happening. Some of the leaders in both labor and religion are actually beginning to listen in new ways. However, much remains to be done. Melissa Snarr presents us with this caution against the top-down spirit: "When worker justice organizing focuses primarily on clergy recruitment and messaging, they replicate many low-wage workers' experience of hierarchy in their job sites and in American political recruitment."[47] Power needs to be built not for working people but by working people. This insight needs to be expanded to include the communities as well.

A grassroots interpretation of the feeding of the four thousand in the New Testament gospels (Mark 8:1–10) takes seriously the agency of the people and illustrates what is at stake. Seven loaves of bread and a few small fish are indeed not sufficient for so many people. Yet what if the point of the story were not the performance of magic but the sharing in which people participate? When the disciples distribute the food to the crowd, the report states that "they ate and were filled" (Mark 8:8). A Philippine nun put it best when she attributed the agency to the women of the community: "What woman," she said, "would leave home for an extended trip without packing some food?" What if the sharing of the disciples inspired the crowd to share the food they brought, so that in the end there was plenty of food for everyone, including seven baskets of leftovers? This would indeed be a great miracle.

With such stories and fuller understanding, labor could learn a great deal from religion.

CHAPTER 6

Organizing and Building the Movement

This chapter is a compilation of steps we have taken in Dallas to bring people of faith and labor together. This project on labor and religion draws on many long discussions we have had over the past thirty-five years. Our experience in trying to bring these two worlds together in our own lives and within the community has been an interesting challenge and we are by no means close to a good finish. This book is our attempt to take the conversations and our hands-on experience to a broader level. It is intended as a discussion primer and we look forward to many more conversations on how to move forward together.

The project has not come about without tensions. While Joerg is a professor of theology, as well as an ordained United Methodist clergy, Rosemarie has left the Christian faith and the church behind after years of disillusionment with where the church is headed and how it tends to treat those who think outside the norm. Her interest in working with faith groups in organizing is pragmatic and appreciative: in order to build power for social and economic justice, we need a mass movement that unites a broad base of society and the best way to organize is to start with people who are already part of groups with defined self-interests that overlap with the broader self-interest of other movements. To a great extent the labor movement and religious communities, as we have shown in previous chapters, have overlapping interests and histories, making them almost natural allies.[1]

Rosemarie's work as an organizer was born in the antinuclear energy movement of the Reagan era during the Cold War. Her first steps in actively becoming involved in the democratic process were taken working with the budding environmental and peace movements, opposing nuclear armament in Europe. As an American teenager living in Germany, she took part in a "human chain" of over three hundred thousand people, holding hands between two cities roughly sixty miles apart. It was one of the most powerful experiences in her life and was the start of her quest to be a part of a larger movement for social and economic justice.

Joerg was there next to her in the human chain, and since then the two of us have spent many hours reflecting on how we can make an impact as individuals and as part of a larger movement to make the struggle for a new world part of our daily fabric. After spending years in the lab as a molecular biologist, and then as a Montessori teacher and homeschool educator, she came to the labor movement as an activist/member of Jobs with Justice. This was the only organization in Dallas that had a long-term vision for social and economic change, and it brought together labor and community organizations, faith groups, and students. The two of us agreed with the need to shift the balance of power for a just and sustainable world and wanted to play an active role. We spent many years participating and Rosemarie eventually took on a leadership role with Jobs with Justice (JwJ). Once our daughters were off to college she was ready to become engaged in this work full-time. She became a full-time organizer and worked for JwJ and the Dallas AFL-CIO as the community engagement coordinator.

Jobs with Justice is a national organization made up of forty-five autonomous local coalitions in twenty-four states. It is a coalition of labor and community groups who believe all workers—not just the ones who are fortunate enough to be organized in unions—should have collective bargaining rights, employment security, and a decent standard of living. The Dallas area chapter was founded by Gene and Elaine Lantz in the early 1990s. Gene and Elaine have been reminding us that change does not come overnight and that it is hard work. By offering points of contact through action (solidarity actions, pickets, protests, marches, educational evenings, etc.), we create opportunities to educate others and encourage them to be a part of the struggle for change.

The principles of our work are putting people over profits, organizing from the bottom up confronting power through direct action, uniting and taking on struggles no one could win alone, addressing root causes through strategic campaigns, and winning campaigns.[2] Jobs with Justice calls on members to "turn out at least 5 times a year for someone's struggle." It is part of a pledge card that all people are invited to sign.[3] We see the pledge as a first step on the road to deep solidarity.

The Importance of Organizing and Deep Solidarity

In this chapter we come back to the insight that nothing will change without organizing the collective power of people. Just like the problems that we are up against are not natural catastrophes but were produced by powerful moneyed interests, the solutions will come from people putting pressure on leaders to change economic policies and embrace social justice and keeping the heat on as long as necessary. Organizing is the essence of movement building and is most effective when it feeds into movements, connects them, and propels them forward. Working people are most powerful when we work towards similar goals, keeping our eyes on the same prize, realizing no one can do it alone. Together we are stronger!

We have come to the conclusion that the basis for any kind of broad-based movement is deep solidarity. This is what connects us, this is where our self-interests overlap. Without deep solidarity there can be no movement that can be sustained over the long haul. And if history has taught us one thing, it is that change does not happen overnight. In this context, we often think about the quote on a postcard on Rosemarie's desk credited to an Aboriginal activist group (Queensland, 1970s): "If you have come here to help me, you are wasting your time. But if you have come because your liberation is bound up with mine, then let us work together." This is at the core of deep solidarity: knowing that your struggle and your liberation is part of ours and vice versa.

This chapter is based on our Dallas experience on the ground, which poses particular challenges. It goes without saying that what we are describing here is for the most part empirical. Part of the challenge is that being located in Dallas means to live and organize in the South where most working people are religious. At the same time, religion in the South often opposes labor. When we ask working people whether they talk about matters of work, labor, and union organizing in their faith communities, the answer is often negative. Many working people assume that religion opposes labor and hardly anyone expects that the struggles of work and labor will find a positive response in their religious organizations.[4]

Furthermore, while it is necessary to build a broad movement that includes advocates and workers, many other groups such as worker centers are finding that particularly low-wage workers have little time between jobs, child-care duties, and commuting to engage in membership activities. This results in solidarity actions and campaigns planned and executed by staff with little or no participation of workers themselves.[5]

Whose Side Are You On?

Just as people of faith need an adequate theology to become open for deep solidarity, people also need an adequate economic consciousness or class consciousness, if you will, to see clearly how their own economic realities line up. It really boils down to the question: Whose side are you on?

One way to visualize this is to draw a number line from 0 to 9,000,000. Mark your wealth and then see if you are closer to the median household wealth of $121,000 or to the wealth of the top 1 percent, namely $8,400,000.[6] According to the *Guardian,* the share of wealth owned by the top 0.1 percent is almost equal to all the wealth shared by the bottom 90 percent.[7]

Another reality check is to consider the possibility of upward mobility. Whose side are you moving toward? More and more people, when asked this question, are responding the American Dream is not attainable and the numbers prove them right.[8] So in one sense it is all about the numbers. Another way to look at it, somewhat simplistically, is that if you have to work to support yourself and your family then you are a worker. Most of us, at least 99 percent, fall into this category. So whose side are you on?

If you still are not clear on this, consider your power at work. Do you have the power to significantly determine or influence your pay, working hours, working conditions, benefits, how resources are used, what is produced or what service is provided, etc.? Few of us are in such a position. It is often overlooked that the heart of the problem is not money but power.

The larger the group that recognizes they might be benefiting from a fight to improve the conditions for workers in all sectors, the broader and stronger the labor movement of the future will be and the greater our chances to make a difference. We cannot win this alone; we need a broad base as our foundation for building power to fight for economic justice. As the saying goes, there are only two types of power in the world: the power of organized money and the power of organized people. As we realize that the proverbial 1 percent hold the power of organized money, our contribution as community and labor organizers is to build power by organizing people. [9]

Bringing Faith and Labor Together[10]

In order to organize people we must bring them together; in order to accomplish this there needs to be some kind of motivation. Self-interest is a first step that can motivate and help us determine why we want or need change. Keep in mind that self-interest is not the same as selfishness or self-centeredness. Under the conditions of deep solidarity, self-interests overlap and keep each other in check. Self-interest is now related to communal interests.

How do we help people understand that their self-interests are related and that they are in the same boat? When people are fighting for change together with others, they are beginning to realize that certain changes will benefit not only themselves but the community as a whole.[11] In due time they begin to realize that they are not alone in this. Their struggle is not just their problem but part of the economic fabric of the neoliberal capitalist system. In this system, as we have seen, profit is maximized by keeping worker pay as low as possible, reducing benefits, pitting workers against each other, keeping workers underemployed, in short by keeping workers unorganized. In an increasing number of cases, even illegal practices such as the misclassification of workers and wage theft are being used in order to maximize profits. Wages stolen in the United States are substantially greater than all things stolen combined (see chap. 2).

Here are some of the actions and events to bring people of faith and the community together around worker rights issues.[12] As we organize together, both the communities of faith and the communities of labor are transformed, creating new energy for real change.

The Workers' Rights Board (WRB)

A Workers' Rights Board is typically made up of concerned local leaders, representing a broad spectrum of the community. The WRB draws together the power of clergy, elected officials, academics, and other community leaders to attract broader public attention to an issue and to create local public awareness. In Dallas, we have used an annual WRB hearing held every Labor Day Weekend to invite people of faith in particular to learn more about specific worker justice issues. Hearing the stories of struggles that workers face on the job has made a significant impression. Over the past nine years we have touched on many topics such as wage theft and wage depression, health care, implications of low-wage jobs, child poverty, health and safety issues on the job, and more. Little of this information is made available through the media in Texas, and one of our efforts is always to invite the media and the press to our events.

We have designed the WRB hearings to be the space where deep solidarity can develop. Hearing the stories of fellow workers gives the audience the opportunity to empathize with the speaker on the one hand and to realize that our struggles and lives are linked on the other hand. The two parts are always related in order to move people from well-meaning acts of advocacy to deep solidarity. Participants realize that the struggle of other workers is their struggle: "Your struggle is my struggle." Or as the labor movement saying goes: "An injury to one is an injury to all." This is a part of the overall message at our hearings.

Our WRB is decidedly pro-worker and provides a collective and unified voice in support of workers, in response to the fact that the playing field has shifted so dramatically in favor of big business and profit. Faced with adversity not only at work but also in many other public spaces, workers need a space that supports their causes. In response to the hearings, the WRB undertakes a range of activities including writing letters and making delegation visits to management or relevant public officials to request positive action; appearing on television or radio programs to publicize worker causes; speaking at press conferences, writing press releases and letters to the editor; and demonstrating solidarity with workers at rallies and other public actions. The past three years we have augmented the hearings with a Labor Day march and a rally and picnic to further highlight the causes addressed at the hearing. This gives participants the chance to act in solidarity immediately following the hearing.

The most important benefit of the Workers' Rights Board is the community support and power it provides for particular workers in the midst of campaign struggles. But there are other benefits as well. The WRB seeks to raise consciousness in the community about the centrality of workers to their communities and the extent to which abuses of workers' rights impact everyone in the community. It seeks to increase community awareness of the positive social role played by labor organizations such as unions and worker centers, and it contributes to the ability of unions and community groups to work together toward common goals. Furthermore, the WRB provides much-needed publicity for labor issues that are often underrepresented in the media. And most importantly, it increases awareness on the part of everyone involved of the profound long-term benefits of building deep solidarity.

For many people the leap to the picket line is too much of a stretch and well outside their comfort zone. As a result, we created a space for deep solidarity to occur outside of protests and pickets and marches. We found that inviting workers to tell their stories of their struggles at the workplace was the perfect venue. At these WRB hearings, we specifically invite people of faith and religious leaders to listen to the testimony of particular workers, with the goal of helping them understand that the struggles of these workers is our struggle too. When one group of workers is kept down, the rights of all workers as well as their wages, benefits, and their value are undermined. In this safe space, probing questions can be posed, real-life stories can be told, and honest conversations become possible. Deep solidarity can be formed. It has taken time, but we are seeing an increase in attendance at the hearings, as well as at key solidarity events.

Unlike other WRBs in other cities, our board is made up of members of the community, not just of selected members with certain leadership functions. We do, however, at times target faith leaders, academics, and community leaders to write letters, make phone calls, and meet with corporate leaders to practice deep solidarity by advocating for workers in need when it is necessary to put pressure on the target. Joerg and several other pastors have met, for instance, with CEOs and the legal teams and so enabled workers to get a meeting with management. Without this support, workers, especially Latino workers, are often ignored and would never get a chance to talk to management face to face. This is one example of how deep solidarity works. Using one's privilege such as the respect and power that come with being a (white) pastor in support of undocumented workers is a first step to deconstruct white privilege. The result is not only the improvement of the conditions of workers—even though results are not always guaranteed—but the transformation of the pastors and activists who enter into relations of deep solidarity.

Solidarity Actions

In the past, when we were a smaller, all-volunteer Jobs with Justice chapter we mainly supported worker/union-led actions when we were called. This is also known as the "cheap date" or "rent-a-rally" model. While it worked to mobilize activists to get out in the streets to stand up for workers' rights when community support was needed, this type of action did not greatly help to expand our base. As a cheap date we also never had input into planning the actions nor were we part of the leadership team making the decisions.

On the other hand, these actions were perfect to get our members involved and educated on the challenges many workers face on the job. We also used these actions to make good on the Jobs with Justice pledge of being there for someone else's struggle at least five times a year. Despite the limitations, these were truly solidarity building blocks. While we never were able to mobilize huge crowds, there were always about ten to twenty people who showed up for actions and to whom local unions were thankful for being the steadfast community representatives. Among the supporters were, not surprisingly, several clergy and people of faith.

Another type of solidarity action with people of faith we have organized is invitations to open prayer circles. With our "Change Walmart, Change the Economy" campaign, prayer circles turned out to be very successful. During one Walmart in-store action, clergy and some members of various faith groups formed an impromptu prayer circle at the front of the store. After joining hands and bowing their heads, the participants took turns saying short unrehearsed prayers for Walmart workers. Many customers stopped on their way out of the store to see what was going on and listened intently. Through the prayers spoken out loud, the public was educated on the unjust working conditions at Walmart. For people of faith who witnessed the event, this was most likely the first occasion to witness religion at work in support of working people.

Once security was called and the demonstrators were ordered to leave the store, management was still at a loss on how to break up the prayer circle. The power of this event was symbolized by the managers pacing around the circle in frustration, looking for some kind of opening to shut it down. Soon after this incident Walmart filed an injunction barring Jobs with Justice from entering stores except for shopping purposes, so we were never able to repeat this type of action inside the store. Two of the prayer circle participants were OUR Walmart members and workers at other stores. They absolutely felt empowered by this action.

Another action that helped bring in new faces and voices to the fight for workers was using songs at rallies. When we announced a practice session through social media, we were amazed when a local street choir that we did not know contacted us. In a place like Dallas, one tends to know one's allies. This choir was made up of members of various local Unitarian Universalist churches and they wanted to sing at protests, but did not yet know how to get involved. Together we practiced some old movement favorites such as "Solidarity Forever" and "This Little Light of Mine" and took our performance to a nearby Walmart one Saturday morning in November. We got some press attention and made passers-by aware of the Black Friday strikes happening at Dallas area stores in the next week.

We invited the choir to sing at the Black Friday Walmart event but were taken by surprise when the choir tried to sing during the chants of the workers. After some diplomatic inquiries we found out that the choir members found chanting to be a violent action and their goal was to set a peaceful tone to the gathering. In a quick conversation we were able to make it clear that in order to support the workers it is necessary to unify against the violence of corporations such as Walmart, not tone-down the anger and disappointment of the striking workers. When these ground rules were understood we had a great rally with alternating song and chanting, speeches and prayers.

Many people later commented on how the singing of the choir had brought a new dimension to our action and how they appreciated the unifying nature of song. The choir members also began to realize what is sometimes difficult for people of faith to see: expressions of anger and even conflict are not always inappropriate and unacceptable. The prophets of the Hebrew Bible, Jesus, and the Prophet Muhammad did not condemn righteous anger; at times they employed it themselves. According to the Qur'an, "Permission [to fight] has been given to those who are being fought, because they were wronged. And indeed, Allah is competent to give them victory" (22:39). Now we make a point to invite the choir to marches and protests and we have song sheets prepared for sing-alongs. One of the members of Jobs with Justice in Dallas, Jann Aldredge-Clanton, is a hymn writer who has written several religion and labor hymns and songs.[13]

Songs also help to remind us of past movements, such as the civil rights movement, and they remind us of the victories of the movement. The songs bring to mind that we stand on the shoulders of many courageous activists and people of faith. And we stand with many others who are fighting for civil rights and human rights, against growing economic inequality, the devaluation of work and the erosion of worker rights, increasing poverty, large-scale environmental damage, war, etc., all over the globe. Actions with global impact such as the 1999 "Battle in Seattle" against the World Trade organization solidified many coalitions between labor, environmental groups, human rights organizations, students, and people of faith.[14] It is comforting to know that we have never been alone in this struggle even though it might sometimes feel that way. All the advances that working people enjoy, including eight-hour workdays, weekends off work, protections for women and children, benefits, were won by people standing up for better and more just working conditions all over the world.

The Peer Chaplains Program

The Peer Chaplains Program is another example of a program that we deployed to encourage faith and labor to work together and to make use of the substantial resources that faith communities bring to the table. This program is related to Alexia Salvatierra's work on matters of religion and labor and her model of faith-based organizing.[15] In our case, all participants were Christians but this project is also applicable to interreligious and interfaith contexts.

With this program we engaged Walmart workers as part of the "Change Walmart, Change the Economy" campaign to read and study selected biblical passages and stories with a group of local pastors, academics, and theology students. The participants analyzed their own faith-rooted motivations for standing up for justice and were encouraged to use their faith to inspire, lead, and organize their colleagues in the struggle for their rights as workers.

This program is based on our understanding that religious and labor communities have much to offer to each other and that this relation helps each of them deepen their work. The key questions we ask in this program are: How can faith help in our everyday struggles at work? How can faith help us in our struggles against economic injustice? And: How do our experiences at work and on the job shape our faith?

To answer these questions we first reached out to Walmart workers and began a journey to help workers and mentors understand their faith in the context of work and the day-to-day struggles they face. Identifying the biblical call to economic justice and building on it gives participants the energy to sustain the struggle and work for justice and it motivates workers to do and to seek justice for themselves and for their coworkers. Since most workers in the South are people of faith, this program also helps workers to inspire fellow workers to join the struggle. Faith can be the driving force for action leading to change at work, at home, and even in the religious communities to which the participants belong.

Walmart workers have been organizing for years to hold their company accountable to a higher standard of corporate responsibility. As the largest retailer in the world, with revenues at $485 billion in 2014,[16] Walmart sets the standard for labor practices globally. While Walmart workers are unionized in Europe, South America, Japan, and South Africa, the company is fighting back and retaliating against workers in the United States for standing up for better working conditions and pay. These workers live in constant fear of losing their jobs while taking the risk of fighting back for justice.

For many of these workers, their faith in a God who cares about justice and who takes the side of the oppressed is an important force enabling them to overcome their fear. As the pressure at work for their involvement intensifies, workers benefit from religious support deeply rooted in their faith traditions. In this program, workers develop their own agency based on their own interpretation of their own faith. The Peer Chaplains project is designed to equip Walmart workers to serve as peer chaplains to help and support their fellow workers during disputes with management, unfair labor practices, and other issues.

Pastors, academics, and students working with the program as allies of the workers offer resources such as training and mentoring, Bible studies, and discussion groups that investigate the religious calls to economic justice in specific situations at work. Through this interaction, the peer chaplains develop an understanding of the processes and mechanics of oppression that they experience at work, and they deepen their already existing ability to engage other workers in discussions about worker and economic justice from a faith perspective. Both the peer chaplains and their allies learn in the process. As the peer chaplains learn, they pass on what they have learned and they begin to analyze their own motivations for standing up for justice and help their coworkers discover theirs. The allies also learn as the workers help them see central aspects of their faith in new light.

This program is beneficial for all workers interested in connecting their faith with a way of seeking justice on the job, leading to a more profound understanding of organizing and the realization that only when workers organize do they have a chance of winning. Especially in the South where religion and faith play such a great role in the lives of so many people, engaging religious traditions in light of everyday experiences at work is powerful. While religion is often used to shore up the dominant powers—Walmart itself uses religious themes to influence workers—religion can also help transform the status quo, which is often the more genuine use of religion. In our experience, reading the Bible in the midst of the pressures of everyday life naturally brings to light the problems and the potential of working people: throwing new light on power differentials at the workplace opens the door for many discussions on how to resist and how to make a difference. Such far-ranging discussions would be very difficult to start in many other contexts.

After offering several trainings we have experienced that there is a hunger among workers and organizers to connect their faith with their everyday work. We have had many lively discussions and the groups were always very grateful for creating such spaces. In the process, we have learned a great deal about how religion functions and what difference it makes. Religion, even when it means well and tries to help, also needs to be deepened. In response to conversations about the tensions between the 1 percent and the 99 percent, for instance, religion is often used to emphasize the unity of all people, the 100 percent. Unfortunately, such harmony is an illusion in the world of working people, who have very limited power over shaping their own lives. Questions like whether people have enough money this week for food and rent, whether they can figure out the child-care situation next week when the schedule will be different again, whether they will get enough hours this month to make ends meet, whether they can pay off medical bills and whether they will be able to send their children to college, matter not only to survival but also to a deeper understanding of life.

Many have not yet heard that work matters to God[17], and that the God of the Abrahamic traditions does not shy away from addressing the struggles of the 99 percent working majority—while inviting the 1 percent to join the struggle for a better life for all. When the difference between the 1 percent and the 99 percent is overlooked, the mistaken notion persists that all have equal opportunity to shape their own destinies and that all of us have come as far as we have by pulling ourselves up by our own bootstraps.

This is just one example of how developing fresh readings of religious traditions in the midst of everyday struggles is a powerful experience for all who participate. On several occasions the participants in our Peer Chaplains program noted that the Bible seems to come alive most powerfully when read in the union halls and on the street.

None of this work happens by default. What we have learned is that labor and faith groups need to make the clear "ask" of their members—both people of faith and the rank-and-file of the unions—to join the movement for social and economic change. Both labor and faith are still too self-centered, focused only on their members and their narrow concerns, and both benefit from seeing beyond their internal problems. The connection between faith and labor needs to be made purposefully. We have many identities, but there is one identity almost all of us have in common: we're defined by work.

Building Coalitions: No One Can Do It Alone

As we already examined, deep solidarity helps to move us beyond our self-centeredness. Once we realize that our struggles and fates are intrinsically linked and that no one wins unless we all win, we can take the next step of building purposeful relationships. The term purposeful relationship might at first sound idealistic and superficial, but it is all about honoring each other's commitments, needs, self-interests, and capacities. When we do that, we can intentionally make connections based on a strategic analysis of the problem and together work towards a solution—or even better, a victory for all.[18]

Building coalitions is hard work! That is probably one of the reasons why we shied away from it for so long. When Rosemarie got involved in the Dallas justice scene around 2006, hardly anyone worked together. We all had our own group's self-interest at heart and supported that work. Jobs with Justice's mission is to connect groups and build coalitions around worker rights issues, so we would invite groups to our actions and we became more open to planning with others. But it was rarely, if ever, reciprocated. We then started cosponsoring each other's events and cross-posted to social media. This was a good start but it was impossible to attend all the events going on. There was also no cohesion between our support for one issue and the next, from protesting war crimes, to Medicare expansion, to saving the bees—all in one week.[19]

We want and need a broad movement, but how do we combine our passions without giving up what we see as most important, like racial justice, marriage equality, women's rights, labor rights, peace, civil rights, LGBTQ rights, environmental justice, etc.? In order to bring the various groups together, we needed something so big and so bad that it would unite us all! We did not have to wait too long for an opportunity to present itself.

ALEC, the American Legislative Exchange Coalition, came to Dallas in the summer of 2014 and we put together a great coalition in just a few months. The coalition, "Don't Mess with Texas, ALEC," was made up of labor and community groups with a few pastors and faith groups mixed in. Putting forward a unified message, pooling resources, determining leadership roles, and getting at-large member buy-in took a lot of work and a lot of patience. In the end, "Don't Mess with Texas, ALEC" was a great success with five hundred people coming together from all over the state and beyond, including some from faith groups playing supportive roles.

ALEC's method of privately working out state legislation benefiting corporations with elected officials and corporate lobbyists is antidemocratic and immoral. "Stand your ground" and voter ID laws are two examples of ALEC's work. Stand your ground law says that you can use deadly force to protect yourself even outside your home if you believe that someone wants to harm or kill you. This law came to public attention during the Trayvon Martin case in Florida in 2013.[20] Texas, along with over thirty other states, has enacted voter ID laws requiring that voters show some form of government issued ID at the polls. The claim is that this type of law will prevent voter impersonation, a crime that is extremely rare.[21] What the law does instead is put hardship and costs on poor and elderly voters who often do not have a driver's license or passport.

ALEC's ways of undermining democracy and lack of morality generated broad concern, resulting in people of faith joining the coalition of civil rights groups, unions, community groups, retirees, environmentalists, and others in collective outrage. With public protests building, several large corporations left ALEC within the next couple of weeks. Our coalition was also encouraged to learn that people all over the United States have been keeping the pressure on ALEC wherever their meetings take place and that the group is losing power as more and more large businesses jump ship.

After ALEC left town, our next challenge was to keep the momentum going and keep everyone, including people of faith, actively involved in the coalition. Our next project was to form a community and labor table and engage a broad coalition in a strategic fight. This was part of the so-called Southern Strategy that the national AFL-CIO has conceptualized for five cities in the south. With the help of the Partnership for Working Families and various AFL-CIO organizers who had many years' experience in coalition building and site-fights, Communities United for a Greater Dallas was founded as a coalition of various groups. We are currently working on a campaign to bring a full-service grocery store to one of Dallas's food deserts in the southern region of the city, which would provide not only fresh produce but also good jobs and fair wages under unionization. In addition, the project should also bring good jobs for local residents during the building and operational phases. This way of building "people power" is all new territory for us in Dallas.[22] Faith communities have also shown interest and we look forward to working with the local PICO affiliate, Faith in Texas, as well as our Jobs with Justice faith allies.

Judging from other recent campaigns this will not be an easy win! A local worker center that campaigned for a "rest break" ordinance learned the hard way that Dallas is no easy place. Intended to grant construction workers just a ten-minute rest break for every four hours worked, the regulation was strongly opposed by real estate councils and builders associations. An interfaith group partnering with the worker center in negotiations wanted an ordinance without a clear path of enforcement to try and keep the builders happy. Thankfully the worker center and various labor groups pulled the ordinance. It finally passed in late 2015, two years after the efforts started, when it was reintroduced to a newly elected city council.

This win was possible because the new council is more worker-friendly thanks to the involvement of community organizing groups and labor in the elections. These groups made sure that their members were well educated on the issues of the election, identifying those candidates who stood for working families and endorsing candidates who went through screening and a rigorous survey process. In addition, the groups also offered training for candidates on issues that are important to the communities.

In our experience faith communities are drawn to those campaigns that have moral implications. Matters of injustices by our capitalist economic system are less likely to resonate. Faith communities tend to engage in actions that have more of a reform character and issues such as predatory lending practices can mobilize hundreds. Faith communities are often hesitant to address the systemic sins inherent in capitalism. There is a notion that if consumers were better protected and lenders had more stringent guidelines, the problems of working people would take care of themselves. The question of why so many are left with no choice but to use payday lenders and why this has become prevalent is not being addressed by most faith communities.

Pushback

Determining who is the opposition is an important part of analyzing the power structures. And when working on labor issues the opposition is definitely powerful. Dallas area companies have spent hundreds of thousands of dollars hiring union-busting firms during union-election processes. These firms put together videos and other materials to dissuade workers from forming a bargaining collective. Corporations require mandatory one-on-one meetings with workers and promises are made in return for not voting for the union. Worker leaders are often harassed, threatened, and sometimes fired for minor work-related issues or for no reason at all.[23] So-called captive audience meetings that workers must attend are held regularly. At the same time, all the organizing work that unions do has to take place after hours and often off-site, making it difficult to reach all the workers.[24]

The way to counter these negative forces is called *inoculation*. Union organizers prepare the workers for the employers' comeback lines and the increasingly escalating force of company pushback. This is why we included the topic of overcoming lies in our Peer Chaplains program, which is also part of Alexia Salvatierra's Peer Chaplains program mentioned above. During one of our sessions with our peer chaplains we talked with workers and organizers about their experiences of lies that come from the top and how these lies forge the divide between workers. Exposing the lies told at work and confronting them with the truth is one of the most foundational discussions for connecting faith and labor. For instance, when workers who have been told directly or indirectly that they do not matter discover that they do matter to their communities and to God, things begin to change.

Of all the discussion we have had on intersections of faith and labor with working people and organizers, our conversations on lies and the connection to union-busting engage them the most. Everyone has a story to share of half-truths and outright lies they were told—"the company cares about you," "we are like a family here," "we will give you a raise," "we were just waiting for you to tell us what you need," "just come to me when you have a problem," "you can tell me anything." The point of these conversations is to detect and anticipate the lies because the corporate bottom line benefits from the deception of workers. We use our connectedness to each other (deep solidarity) and our investigations of truth in the midst of lies to keep up the courage when times are tough and to stay determined to work for what is right, what we deserve, and what we want to improve, so that the rights of all working people are respected.

Lawsuits

At Jobs with Justice we have had our own encounter with corporate pushback with Walmart, as we described in chapter 2. It is a "David and Goliath" story of a small community, faith, and labor coalition facing the corporate behemoth. The actions of Walmart were, of course, just tactics used to decrease the movement's energy by tying up resources, intimidating organizers and activists, and limiting the capacity so that actions resonating with the broader public cannot be continued at the same scale.

Media Inattention and Boycotts

Media attention to labor struggles has proven to be minimal. While this might be a local problem or the consequence of living in the South, the lack of interest in matters related to workers and their activities is quite evident. While we have been fairly successful in getting the Spanish-speaking news channels to report on the hearings and other campaigns, other news agencies are usually not interested.

Unless there is a provocative action planned such as civil disobedience, news media avoid labor demonstrations, marches, and rallies in Dallas. Our anti-ALEC demonstration that brought together over five hundred activists from the region was boycotted by the media: not a single local mainstream media camera or reporter took notice. We learned to rely on alternative media, experienced first-hand how crucial making our own media is, and engaged in what is now called civic reporting. With the ALEC fight-back, we shared photos, video, reports on social media (Facebook, Twitter, YouTube, targeted e-mail lists, newsletters, etc.), and we received the help of nonmainstream reporters to take the message and spread it through their channels. With many people's cellphone cameras shooting and sharing instantly, word spread widely. Even though local media boycotted the event, national progressive media picked up our stories and shared them.

Getting the media's attention is one thing. Actually getting the message across is another story. Faith leaders with their regalia at actions sometimes do get the attention of the press. Yet it has been our experience that the message faith leaders present in support of worker demands is often cut from the reports. Joerg has been interviewed by local news frequently on why people of faith attend rallies in support of workers, but the religious message of deep solidarity is always removed.

Using alternative media effectively and getting more people involved in these efforts is, therefore, crucial for the whole message to be communicated. And hopefully this will attract increased attention from the mainline media as well.

Reclaiming Our Rights and the Biblical Mandate for Justice

We cannot take the next steps in reclaiming our rights without acknowledging our own economic situation as working people. We don't need to become hobby economists, but we do need to understand the basic principles of how the economy is shaped by policy decisions and not simply the course of nature. The AFL-CIO has done a great job putting together an educational program for members called "Common Sense Economics."

The program is designed to educate union members and community allies on how our economy works and how policies impact our economy. It shows how economic policies are increasingly skewed to benefit a few, rather than the many. It also reveals that this has not always been the case and that policies benefiting workers, such as the eight-hour day, were only implemented after bitter battles and lost lives.[25] Just as many current policies were shaped by the dominant powers, they can be changed to make the economy work for all—women, undocumented, the young, and even the previously incarcerated. All can be treated justly, not just the wealthy few.

Democracy is dangerous to the interests of the elites. When people become involved in the democratic political process they start to understand how power works. They see where the system is rigged against them. So it is no wonder that voting rights are increasingly being suppressed, for instance by passing stringent voter ID laws. Rev. William Barber and the Moral Mondays campaigns in North Carolina have done an excellent job of bringing this and other issues to the front pages of our news sources and showing how faith and labor have an active stake in this.

The same is true for unions and organized labor. If unions did not pose a threat to corporate power then why are they under such attack? The more working people have a say in all aspects relating to our work and the more we have an actual stake in the fruits and profits of our labor, the more we realize how much profit the corporations and big business are making off of our hard work. Since wages have not risen noticeably in several decades, corporations have been able to increase their surplus value on our work significantly. As a result, most of the wealth created in the past decade has gone to the top while middle-class and lower-class wages have stagnated even though worker productivity has increased.[26] This affects all of us whether we are union members or people of faith or both, or neither. We are in the same boat that is not being lifted by rising tides. The claims of the majority of mainline economists ring false to us, as Joerg has pointed out in another book.[27]

The corporate agenda of maximizing profits benefits from keeping unemployment and underemployment high; from deregulating banking, environmental, safety and other controls while privatizing services; from giving tax breaks to the wealthy and corporations; and from raising executive pay while cutting the wages and benefits for workers and attacking unions. This agenda is the foundation for the current global economic system. That is why targeting multinational corporations such as Walmart could potentially have far-reaching consequences for supply chain workers in Mexico, garment workers in Bangladesh, and auto workers in Brazil. As a bumper sticker on our kitchen counter has reminded us for years: "No one is free when others are oppressed."

Nothing will change unless people organize and stand up for change. Hearing the stories of struggle and economic disparity and engaging in action, and standing side-by-side with others in the struggle for economic and social justice are the catalysts needed for transformation and deep solidarity. People of faith fight for justice because God fights for justice—the labor movement and faith communities are uniquely situated to be allies in the fight at all levels, social, economic, and cultural. The values and traditions of both groups encourage us to work to shift decision-making power from the few to a democratic base that empowers all collectively.

For this reason we see the great potential of both of these groups to propel the justice movement forward. We are there for each other's struggles and we unite to take on struggles that none of us can win alone. We build relationships for the long haul that are rooted in the principles of reciprocity, mutual respect, and justice and the conviction that our struggles are linked. This is deep solidarity.

In our work of bringing faith and labor together over the past years we have learned many things from our successes and from our mistakes. Our best examples we have shared here in the hopes that they are useful examples for others to reach out and build a stronger faith and labor coalition. We have come to the conclusion that active involvement with workers' rights issues can no longer be considered optional: our lives and our faith depend on it.

As a result, we need to learn as much as we can about what is going on and educate others, inviting them to join the emerging movements. It all starts at the local level, so we need to link up with local struggles and ask the tough questions in each situation, like "Who is benefiting from this situation?" The good news is that we do not need to reinvent the wheel; we can join forces with existing groups like Jobs with Justice, Interfaith Worker Justice, CLUE, PICO and form alliances with others who are already involved in the struggle. The most important thing to remember, for novices and veterans alike, is that no one can do it alone.

Conclusions

Even though we know that the world is in a profound crisis, deep down many of us continue to share a hope for a better world. Many working people, participants in the labor movements, and some sectors of religion have been energized by this hope for a long time and have made important contributions to the common good. Unfortunately, today many of these contributions are under attack unlike ever before. Some of these attacks are in the open, but many are so well concealed that few people are even aware of them. It is the purpose of this book to build up hope while addressing the severe nature of the crisis and dealing with pushback along the way. Anything less would not contribute to building hope but merely lead us back into frustration, apathy, and paralysis.

If we are correct, religion is not primarily about lofty ideals, flat morality, or merely what people do on weekends. Religion is about building relationships, community, and deep solidarity. Fresh ideals and more authentic morals are evolving in the process. Such religion inspires us to seek the alternative power to the dominant forces at work in the world, and a new way of life for everyone where all work is appreciated and deeply valued.

One of the most critical steps in the march forward is acknowledging the significant contributions of working people and of work to the well-being of the communities. While there is always room for improvement, in many countries workers and their contributions are more highly regarded than in the United States—as indicated by the fact that worker representatives even hold seats on corporate boards in some European countries. If work is to be truly valued, not only do working people deserve to be compensated fairly, they also deserve to have their voices heard and be part of the decision-making process. Yet even in Europe, workers, who are in the majority numerically, are still treated like a minority voice when it comes to corporate and even to political decisions.

Working people do much more than make valuable contributions at the level of production; they also uphold democracy and have the potential to temper the elitist power exercised by corporations. This has happened before, although our collective memory of these matters has been largely erased. Worker benefits like eight-hour workdays, weekends off work, pension plans, and various protections against unfair and unsafe practices were all achieved through the organized power of working people. Churches and religious communities once shared in this power, as many of them supported these causes when they were first fought for over a century ago. Why is it that we remember the accomplishments of the abolitionist, suffragist, and civil rights movements, but not the accomplishments of labor and religion together?

While much of this has been forgotten, today much is happening again. Labor and religion have worked together to various degrees in organizations like Jobs with Justice (JwJ), Interfaith Worker Justice (IWJ), Clergy and Laity United for Economics Justice (CLUE), the AFL-CIO in various states and nationally[1], as well as in many Worker Centers around the country. Genuine interest is growing in how religion and labor issues are related and what we can do together to further the growing relationships.

Progressive Christian groups are emerging that are beginning to take the struggles of working people seriously, groups such as Progressive Christians Uniting, the Dykes Foundation, SPAFER in Birmingham, the Center for Progressive Theology in Houston, and many others.

In the academic world, several progressive schools of theology and religion departments are also beginning to explore religion and labor issues again, including Vanderbilt Divinity School, Syracuse University, Union Theological Seminary in New York, Drew Theological School, Claremont School of Theology, Pacific School of Religion, and Starr King School for the Ministry. Progressive evangelicals are also joining in, including the Transform Network and the Wild Goose Festival.[2] New things are happening even at the level of the national American Academy of Religion, which, despite some initial resistance, now has a working group that deals with matters of class, religion, and theology.

These matters affect us all. This is the most important message of this book, and our irreducible differences should not keep us from recognizing this. For things will only change when more and more of us start working together. Reflecting on deep solidarity can help us get started, but we must continue to explore and discover. We need each other but we are only at the beginning of renewing our relationships after a long period of stagnation. Both religion and labor are at their best when they realize that the transformations to come and currently occurring are bigger than us and greater than either can achieve alone. This is where our hope is rooted.

Notes

Preface

[1]The term *deep solidarity* was coined by Joerg in 2011 in response to the Occupy Wall Street Movement. It is discussed in detail in chapter 3.

[2]We use the terms interchangeably and together with the intention to broaden narrow notions of work and labor. The term *work* is often used as an ideal that ignores harsh realities and struggles, and labor is often limited to technical matters in labor organizing. Using both together acknowledges the conflicting reality people experience in their jobs while still encompassing the full implications of productive power that this reality entails as well.

[3]Regina Montoya, "Poverty is Eating at Dallas' Core," *The Dallas Morning News*, August 18, 2014, http://www.dallasnews.com/opinion/latest-columns /20140818-poverty-is-eating-at-dallas-core.ece. Accessed January 13, 2016.

Acknowledgments

[1]The recording of this event would be an excellent supplement to this book, and it is available from the D.L. Dykes, Jr. Foundation website, http://faithandreason.org/index.php/store/product/houston-confronting-poverty-dvd.

Introduction

[1]Michael Zweig, *The Working Class Majority: America's Best Kept Secret*, 2nd ed. (Ithaca: ILR Press, 2012), 36. According to Zweig, 63 percent of Americans are working class, 35 percent middle class, and 2 percent belong to what he calls the capitalist class. In 2000, when the first edition of Zweig's book was published, he estimated that 62 percent belonged to the working class and 36 percent to the middle class. Michael Zweig, *The Working Class Majority: America's Best Kept Secret* (Ithaca: ILR Press, 2000), 34–35.

[2]Richard A. Greenwald, "Contingent, Transient, and At-Risk: Modern Workers in a Gig Economy," in *Labor Rising: The Past and Future of Working People in America,* ed. Daniel Katz and Richard Greenwald (New York: The New Press, 2012), 112.

[3]See, for instance, the testimonies on this website: westandwiththe99percent. tumblr.com/.

[4]Phil De Muth, "Are you Rich Enough? The Terrible Tragedy of Income Inequality Among the 1 Percent," *Forbes* (November 25, 2013), http://www. forbes.com/sites/phildemuth/2013/11/25/are-you-rich-enough-the-terrible-tragedy-of-income-inequality-among-the-1/.

[5]Martin Luther King, Jr., *"All Labor has Dignity,"* ed. Michael K. Honey, King Legacy Series (Boston: Beacon Press, 2011), 175. From a speech in Memphis, March 18, 1968, to the American Federation of State, County, and Municipal Employees (AFSCME).

[6]A. Philip Randolph, "March on Washington Movement Presents Program for the Negro," in *What the Negro Wants,* ed. Rayford Whittingham Logan (Chapel Hill: University of North Carolina Press, 1944), 141.

[7]See Cynthia Taylor, *A. Philip Randolph: The Religious Journey of an African American Labor Leader* (New York: New York University Press, 2006), 223.

[8]Jewish Rabbi Michael Lerner blasts what he considers materialism, arguing for spirituality instead. See Michael Lerner, "Why the Right Keeps Winning and the Left Keeps Losing," *Tikkun* (November 10, 2014), http://www.tikkun.org/nextgen/why-the-right-keeps-winning-and-the-left-keeps-losing.

Chapter 1: Basic Issues

[1]See Marcellus Andrews, "On Economics and Labor Solidarity," in Katz and Greenwald, *Labor Rising*, 214–15.

[2]This is one of the key critiques of David H. Jensen, *Responsive Labor: A Theology of Work* (Louisville: Westminster John Knox, 2006).

[3]This is what is called "doing theology" in Joerg's line of work.

[4]John Raines and Donna C. Day-Lower, *Modern Work and Human Meaning* (Philadelphia: The Westminster Press, 1986), 85. The authors point out that democracy "depends upon people who do not believe their worth is something they need to prove."

[5]According to the National Center for Employee Ownership, https://www.nceo.org/articles/employee-ownership-100.

[6]Our focus on work keeps in mind the various theologies of disability that temper traditional views of work and success and develop new forms of agency. See, for instance, Sharon Betcher, *Spirit and the Politics of Disablement* (Minneapolis: Fortress Press, 2007).

[7]Most progressives, and even Thomas Piketty, *Capital in the Twenty-First Century* (Cambridge: The Belknap Press of Harvard University, 2014), fall into this trap as well. In Joerg's book *No Rising Tide: Theology, Economics, and the Future* (Minneapolis: Fortress Press, 2009) and elsewhere, he has argued that we need to shift the focus from distribution to production.

[8]In 2007, the top twenty private equity and hedge-fund managers made 22,255 times the pay of an average worker in the United States. Sarah Anderson et al., "Executive Excess 2007," United for a Fair Economy, http://www.faireconomy.org/files/pdf/ExecutiveExcess2007.pdf.

[9]Alyssa Davis and Lawrence Mishel, "CEO Pay Continues to Rise as Typical Workers are Paid Less" (June 12, 2015), Economic Policy Institute website,http://www.epi.org/publication/ceo-pay-continues-to-rise/.

[10]See Jillian Berman, "U.S. Income Inequality Higher than Roman Empire's Levels: Study," *Huffington Post*, December 19, 2011, http://www.huffingtonpost.com/2011/12/19/us-income-inequality-ancient-rome-levels_n_1158926.html.

[11]In many other countries workers and their contributions are much more highly regarded; in some European countries, in fact, worker representatives hold seats on corporate boards, which is one way of acknowledging and honoring the value and wisdom of working people.

[12]This is one of the key points of Darby Kathleen Ray, *Working* (Minneapolis: Fortress Press, 2011).

[13]Paul Lafargue, *The Right to be Lazy: Essays by Paul Lafargue*, ed. Bernard Marszalek (Chicago: Charles H. Kerr, 2011), 85, 89.

[14]Ibid., 46n1.

[15]Kathi Weeks, *The Problem with Work: Feminism, Marxism, Antiwork Politics, and Postwork Imaginaries* (Durham: Duke University Press, 2011), 12.

[16]See also the reflections of one of our friends, Gail Hamner, who is a professor at a prestigious university: http://rsn.aarweb.org/columns/work-and-life-balance.

[17]Joan M. Martin, *More Than Chains and Toil: A Christian Work Ethic of Enslaved Women* (Louisville, Ky.: Westminster John Knox Press, 2000), 146. Ken Estey, *A New Protestant Labor Ethic at Work* (Cleveland: Pilgrim Press, 2002), 1, also notes the problems with a "Protestant work ethic that values hard work but devalues workers."

[18]As a result, Martin, *More Than Chains and Toil*, 152, argues, "the conversation about work and human meaning must be guided by workers, with theologians and ethicists serving only as facilitators and acting as members of the community of faith in solidarity with those dehumanized by exploitative and oppressive work."

[19]Weeks, *The Problem with Work*, 232.

[20]David Bensman, "The Battle Over Working Time: A Countermovement against Neoliberalism," *American Prospect*, http://prospect.org/article/fair-work-schedules-next-new-human-right.

[21]David Crouch, "Efficiency Up, Turnover Down: Sweden Experiments with Six-Hour Working Day, *The Guardian*, September 17, 2015, http://www.theguardian.com/world/2015/sep/17/efficiency-up-turnover-down-sweden-experiments-with-six-hour-working-day.

[22]LaFargue, *The Right to be Lazy*, 51.

[23]Ibid., 24.

[24]Michael Payne, "Unionization: A Private Sector Solution to the Financial Crisis, *Dissent* (Spring 2009), 59.

[25]See the example of Organization United for Respect at Walmart (OUR Walmart), forrespect.org.

[26]Article 23.4 of the United Nations' Universal Declaration of Human Rights states: "Everyone has the right to form and to join trade unions for the protection of his interests." On the web: http://www.un.org/en/documents/udhr/.

[27]Several of the Papal Encyclicals explicitly affirm the right of forming unions to collective bargaining, beginning with *Rerum Novarum* of Pople Leo XIII in 1891. Recent popes such as John Paul II, Benedict XVI, and Francis agree. See also the documents compiled in Interfaith Worker Justice, *A Worker Justice Reader: Essential Writings on Religion and Labor* (Maryknoll, NY: Orbis Books, 2010), 79–123. See also these additional sources on the web: http://www.iwj.org/resources/protestantism.

[28]Interfaith Worker Justice, *A Worker Justice Reader*, 98–100.

[29]In this book, we consistently list the three religions in this order, based on their historical age. Judaism emerged first, Christianity came later, and Islam is the youngest religion of the three.

[30]Shahien Nasiripour, "Occupy Buys, Then Cancels, Student Debt," *Huffington Post*, September 17, 2014, http://www.huffingtonpost.com/2014/09/17/occupy-wall-street-student-debt_n_5839174.html. See also: http://rollingjubilee.org/transparency/.

[31]This insight grew at the forefront of religion and labor organizing. See Claude Williams' chart "Jesus and the People" in Cedric Belfrage, *A Faith to Free the People* (New York: The Dryden Press, 1944), 243. See also Bill Troy with Claude Williams, "People's Institute of Applied Religion," in Samuel S. Hill Jr., *On Jordan's Stormy Banks: Religion in the South. A Southern Exposure Profile* (Macon, Ga.: Mercer University Press, 1983), 49–58.

Chapter 2: Work under Attack: Dire Consequences

[1]Already in 1993, Harvard economist Juliet Schor, *The Overworked American: The Unexpected Decline of Leisure* (New York: Basic Books, 1993) examined the history and the causes of a situation where more and more people are working longer and longer hours. In Schor's account, the declining power of unions is part of this development, in contrast to Europe where stronger unions contributed to the reduction of hours at work.

[2]Regina Montoya, "Poverty is Eating at Dallas' Core," *The Dallas Morning News*, August 18, 2014, http://www.dallasnews.com/opinion/latest-columns/20140818-poverty-is-eating-at-dallas-core.ece.

[3]United States Department of Labor, Bureau of Labor statistics,http://www.bls.gov/eag/eag.tx_dallas_msa.htm.

[4]Josh Bivens and Lawrence Mishel, "Understanding the Historic Divergence Between Productivity and a Typical Worker's Pay: Why it Matters and Why It's Real" (September 2, 2015), Economic Policy Institute, http://www.epi.org/publication/understanding-the-historic-divergence-between-productivity-and-a-typical-workers-pay-why-it-matters-and-why-its-real/.

[5]We use this term to describe the current form of capitalism that is characterized by a push for deregulation of corporations and businesses, reduction of responsibilities like taxes, and the socialization of losses through government subsidies to corporations, in addition to the capitalist emphasis on maximizing profit.

[6]Jill Lepore, "Richer and Poorer: Accounting for Inequality," *The New Yorker*, March 16, 2015, http://www.newyorker.com/magazine/2015/03/16/richer-and-poorer. Lepore also notes that income inequality in the United States is greater than in any other democratic country in the world and it is growing. By 2012, the top 1 percent were earning almost 23 percent of the nation's income, up from 11 percent in 1944.

[7]As some observers have pointedly put it, universities, for instance, "no longer collude with big business; they have become increasingly *identical* to business." Benjamin Johnson, Patrick Kavanagh, and Kevin Mattson, *Steal this University: The Rise of the Corporate University and the Academic Labor Movement* (New York: Routledge, 2003), 12.

[8]This pattern has been identified in a study of Chicago's working class churches by Robert Anthony Bruno, *Justified by Work: Identity and the Meaning of Faith in Chicago's Working-Class Churches* (Columbus, Ohio: The Ohio State University Press, 2008), 217.

[9]"The Haves and the Have-Nots: How American Labor Law Denies a Quarter of the Workforce Collective Bargaining Rights," American Rights at Work, http://www.jwj.org/wp-content/uploads/2014/04/havesandhavenots_nlracoverage.pdf.

[10]Supreme Court of the United States, *Citizens United v. FEC*, 2010," https://www.law.cornell.edu/supct/html/08-205.ZS.html.

[11]Supreme Court of the United States, *Burwell v. Hobby Lobby*, 2014, https://www.law.cornell.edu/supremecourt/text/13-354.

[12]"Corporate Personhood," *Wikipedia*. On the web: https://en.wikipedia.org/wiki/Corporate_personhood#cite_ref-4.

[13]Michigan Supreme Court, *Dodge v. Ford Motor Company*, http://www.law.illinois.edu/aviram/Dodge.pdf.

[14]Milton Friedman, "The Social Responsibility of Business Is to Increase Its Profits," *The New York Times Magazine,* September 13, 1970. A copy of the article is available at http://www.colorado.edu/studentgroups/libertarians/issues/friedman-soc-resp-business.html.

[15]Kim Bobo, *Wage Theft in America: Why Millions of Americans Are not Getting Paid—And What We Can Do About It* (New York: New Press, 2009). See also http://www.wagetheft.org/moreinfo/kimsbook/kimsbook.html.

[16]Brad Meixell and Ross Eisenbrey, "An Epidemic of Wage Theft Is Costing Workers Hundreds of Millions of Dollars a Year," September 11, 2014, Economic Policy Institute, http://www.epi.org/publication/epidemic-wage-theft-costing-workers-hundreds/.

[17]See the list of worker centers affiliated with IWJ: http://www.iwj.org/network/workers-centers.

[18]See http://www.workersdefense.org/about-us/achievements-2/.

[19]*Fortune*, on the web: http://fortune.com/fortune500/walmart/.

[20]Courtney Gross, "Is Wal-Mart Worse?" *Gotham Gazette*, February 14, 2011, http://www.gothamgazette.com/index.php/economy/694-is-wal-mart-worse.

[21]See Making Change at Walmart, http://makingchangeatwalmart.org/walmart-and-workers/.

[22]"The Low-Wage Drag on Our Economy: Wal-Mart's Low Wages and Their Effect on Taxpayers and Economic Growth," prepared by the Democratic staff of the U.S. House Committee on Education and the Workforce (May 2013), http://democrats.edworkforce.house.gov/sites/democrats.edworkforce.house.gov/files/documents/WalMartReport-May2013.pdf.

[23]Jillian Berman, "Walmart Store Holding Thanksgiving Food Drive for its Own Members," *The Huffington Post*, November 18, 2013, http://www.huffingtonpost.com/2013/11/18/walmart-food-drive_n_4296618.html.

[24]Bethany Moreton, *To Serve God and Wal-Mart: The Making of Christian Free Enterprise* (Cambridge, MA: Harvard University Press, 2009), 91.

[25]Moreton, *To Serve God and Wal-Mart*, 101, 107, 110. It was the *Wall Street Journal* that described the goals of servant leadership in this way.

[26]See the *Human Rights Watch Report*, https://www.hrw.org/report/2010/09/02/strange-case/violations-workers-freedom-association-united-states-european, detailing the egregious practices of T-Mobile and the efforts taken to prevent unionization.

[27]Jodi Kantor and David Streitfeld, "Inside Amazon: Wrestling Big Ideas in a Bruising Workplace," *The New York Times*, August 15, 2015, http://www.nytimes.com/2015/08/16/technology/inside-amazon-wrestling-big-ideas-in-a-bruising-workplace.html?hp&action=click&pgtype=Homepage&module=second-column-region&region=top-news&WT.nav=top-news&_r=1.

[28]Robert Reich, "The Fraud of 'Family Friendly' Work," *RSN*, August 17, 2015, http://readersupportednews.org/opinion2/277-75/31881-the-fraud-of-qfamily-friendlyq-work.

[29]Steven Greenhouse, "How Walmart Persuades Its Workers Not to Unionize," *The Atlantic*, (June 8, 2015), http://www.portside.org/2015-06-09/how-walmart-persuades-its-workers-not-unionize-0.

[30]Jessica Wohl, "Walmart Files U.S. Labor Charge against Union," *Reuters*, November 16, 2012, http://www.reuters.com/article/2012/11/17/us-walmart-union-idUSBRE8AF1DB20121117.

[31]Hiroko Tabuchi, "Walmart Raising Wage to at Least \$9," *The New York Times*, February 19, 2015, http://www.nytimes.com/2015/02/20/business/walmart-raising-wage-to-at-least-9-dollars.html.

[32]See Bruce Rogers-Vaughn, "Blessed are Those Who Mourn: Depression as Political Resistance," *Pastoral Psychology* 63:4 (August 2014), 503–22. Karen Bloomquist, *The Dream Betrayed: Religious Challenge of the Working Class* (Minneapolis: Fortress Press, 1990), 25, talks about workers' pervasive experience of being controlled or dominated. Working people are defined as those who are under the control of others, resulting in alienation. Not surprisingly, working people do not like to talk about their work, especially in church. "Although there is dignity attached to the fact that one is working, there generally is little inherent meaning or dignity in the work itself" (ibid., 23).

[33]"Was ist die Ermordung eines Mannes gegen die Anstellung eines Mannes?" Bertolt Brecht, "Die Dreigroschenoper III, 9 (Mac)," in: *Gesammelte Werke*, vol. 2 (Frankfurt am Main: Suhrkamp Verlag, 1967), 482. Translation ours.

[34]Estey, *A New Protestant Labor Ethic at Work*, vii.

Chapter 3: From Advocacy to Deep Solidarity: Activism Reborn

[1]The term *deep solidarity* was coined by Joerg in 2011 in response to the Occupy Wall Street Movement, "Occupy Wall Street and Everything Else: Lessons for the Study and Praxis of Religion," *Peace Studies Journal* 5:1 (January 2012): 33–45. For more extended reflections see Joerg Rieger and Kwok Pui-lan, *Occupy Religion: Theology of the Multitude*, Religion in the Modern World (Lanham, MD: Rowman and Littlefield, 2012), and Joerg

Rieger, ed., *Religion, Theology, and Class: Fresh Engagements after Long Silence*, New Approaches to Religion and Power (New York: Palgrave Macmillan 2013). Emphasizing shallow commonalities can cause problems, as Ange-Marie Hancock says in *Solidarity Politics for Millennials: A Guide to Ending The Oppression Olympics* (New York: Palgrage Macmillan, 2011), 67, but we believe the shared pressures of capitalism warrant a deeper look. Hancock's reflections on "deep political solidarity" are helpful, particularly in her insistence that this solidarity is not a matter of altruism and public service. Unfortunately, reflections on oppression along the lines of labor, class, and capitalism do not factor into her account.

[2]Steve Martinot, *The Rule of Racialization: Class, Identity, Governance* (Philadelphia: Temple University Press, 2003), 108–10, talks about an "intermediary control stratum," in which both elites and workers share to some extent. He wrote of the formation of this control stratum with reference to Theodore Allen's two-volume work on *The Invention of the White Race*, in Steve Martinot, *The Machinery of Whiteness: Studies in the Structure of Racialization* (Philadelphia: Temple University Press, 2010), 16–17.

[3]See Michael D. Yates, *Why Unions Matter*, 2nd ed. (New York: Monthly Review Press, 2009), 145–51. For a more detailed account see Philip S. Foner, *Organized Labor and the Black Worker: 1619–1973* (New York: Praeger, 1974).

[4]Yates, *Why Unions Matter*, 151–62.

[5]See, for instance, Jefferson Cowie, *Stayin' Alive: The 1970s and the Last Days of the Working Class* (New York: The New Press, 2010).

[6]Fred Rose, *Coalitions Across the Class Divide: Lessons from the Labor, Peace, and Environmental Movements* (Ithaca: Cornell University Press, 2000), 25.

[7]Cowie, *Stayin' Alive*, 367.

[8]Rose, *Coalitions Across the Class Divide*, 30, comments that "divisions between the working and middle classes have consistently undermined progressive politics in the United States."

[9]The Tanakh is widely associated with what Christians call the Old Testament but there are differences including numbering, order, punctuation, and on some occasions there are additional texts like the apocryphal writings that some Christian communities acknowledge. In this book, we will use the text from the New Revised Standard Edition of the Christian Bible, which is common practice among Jewish studies scholars. For comparison, see also the Jewish Publication Society Translation of the Tanakh.

[10]In his "Thoughts on the Present Scarcity of Provisions" of 1772, Wesley talks about various causes of poverty, including the monopolizing of farms by the "gentlemen-farmers" and the luxury of the wealthy. *The Works of the Rev. John Wesley*, ed. Thomas Jackson, 3rd ed. (London: Wesleyan Methodist Book Room, 1872; repr. Peabody, MA: Hendrickson, 1986), 11:56–57.

[11]Zildo Rocha, *Helder, O Dom: uma vida que marcou os rumos da Igreja no Brasil* (Sao Paulo: Editora Vozes, 2000), 53.

[12]This is one of the problems with the so-called dependency theory.

[13]Darren Cushman Wood, "The Church, The Union, and the Trinity," in Interfaith Worker Justice, *A Worker Justice Reader: Essential Writings on Religion and Labor*, 198. Similar questions are also raised in several of the books of Tex Sample.

[14]See Jan Rehmann, "Poverty and Poor People's Agency in High-Tech Capitalism," in Rieger, ed., Religion, Theology, and Class, 147–52. See also Guy Standing, *The Precariat: The New Dangerous Class* (London: Bloomsbury Academic, 2011).

[15]One way to illustrate the difference is to consider that a million seconds is 13 days, while a billion seconds is 31 years. For million dollars in $100 bills, a backpack would do. For a billion dollars, ten forklifts would be necessary. A nice graphical illustration of this difference can be found in Mick Weinstein,

"The difference between a million and a billion (with graphic)," July 12, 2012, *Smarter Investing,*http://investing.covestor.com/2012/07/the-difference-between-a-million-and-a-billion-dollars-graphic.

[16]The reference is to the heirs of Sam Walton, the founder of Walmart. Tom Kertscher, "Just How Wealthy is the Wal-Mart Walton Family?" *Politifact Wisconsin,* December 8, 2013, http://www.politifact.com/wisconsin/statements/2013/dec/08/one-wisconsin-now/just-how-wealthy-wal-mart-walton-family/.

[17]Thanks to Jewish studies scholar Santiago Slabodsky, who encouraged us to broaden the perspective beyond Moses.

[18]See the work of Norman K. Gottwald, *The Tribes of Yahweh: A Sociology of the Religion of Liberated Israel 1250–1050 B.C.E.* (Maryknoll, NY: Orbis Books, 1979). In other words, while these texts have sometimes been used to endorse colonialism and occupation—for instance by contemporary Israel of Palestine—this seems to be a misuse.

[19]According to Jewish scholar Aryeh Cohen, "'And Demand Justice': A Jewish Response to the Business of Poverty," in Interfaith Worker Justice, *A Worker Justice Reader,* 154, the law obligates people of the Jewish faith to be like God, which in this case means to hear those who cry out and not to be like Pharaoh, namely to ignore them.

[20]While such trade associations shared both similarities and differences with modern labor unions, what is important is that they developed forms of solidarity and community that helped them deal with the challenges of everyday work. See Jonathan Draper, "Christ the Worker: Fact or Fiction?" In *The Three-Fold Cord: Theology, Work and Labour,* ed. James R. Cochrane and Gerald O. West (Pietermaritzburg: Cluster Publications, 1991), 123-24.

[21]Richard A. Horsley, *Covenant Economics: A Biblical Vision of Justice for All* (Louisville KY: Westminster John Knox Press, 2009), points out that the term enemies was commonly used in the covenantal imagery of Jesus' time for neighbors with whom local communities had come into conflict (110).

[22]Draper, "Christ the Worker," 139, comes to a similar conclusion in his discussion of Jesus as worker.

[23]Ben Stein, "In Class Warfare, Guess Which Class is Winning," *The New York Times,* November 26, 2006, http://www.nytimes.com/2006/11/26/business/yourmoney/26every.html?_r=0.

[24]There may be an advantage to talking about work as that which connects us, rather than class. Unlike class, work cannot be understood as a fixed identity: work is always dynamic, in process. See Kathi Weeks, *The Problem with Work: Feminism, Marxism, Antiwork Politics, and Postwork Imaginaries* (Durham: Duke University Press, 2011), 17, on that issue.

[25]Marcellus Andrews, "On Economics and Labor Solidarity," in *Labor Rising: The Past and Future of Working People in America,* ed. Daniel Katz and Richard A. Greenwald (New York: The New Press, 2012), 219. "Narrow labor solidarity creates the conditions for its own demise by establishing pools of excluded and angry outsiders who are more than willing to oust their privileged racial or ethnic enemies from their good wages and working conditions by offering a much less demanding labor bargain to capital" (ibid).

[26]Ibid., 223.

[27]One might also talk about class solidarity at this point. The same lesson applies however: class solidarity does not mean being identical (sameness) but being able to put your differences to use. See Joerg Rieger, "Instigating Class Struggle? The Study of Class in Religion and Theology in the United States And Some Implications for Race and Gender," in *Religion, Theology, and Class,* 189–211.

[28]We agree with Hancock, *Solidarity Politics for Millennials,* 127, that "allowing privilege to remain invisible facilitates the Oppression Olympics."

[29]W. E. B. Du Bois, *Writings by W.E.B. Du Bois in Periodicals Edited by Others,* vol. 4, collated and ed. Herbert Aptheker (Millwood, NY: Kraus-Thomson Organization, 1982), 68. The comment praises the CIO, founded in 1935.

[30]Dorothy Day, *The Long Loneliness* (New York: Harper 1952). The quote is from the introduction by Robert Coles (1997), 3.

[31]These numbers are published by the American Association of University Women (AAUW), http://www.aauw.org/2014/09/18/gender-pay-gap/.

[32]C. Melissa Snarr, *All You That Labor: Religion and Ethics in the Living Wage Movement,* Religion and Social Transformation (New York: New York University Press, 2011), 154.

[33]Elizabeth A. Johnson, "Redeeming the Name of Christ," in *Freeing Theology: The Essentials of Theology in Feminist Perspective,* ed. Catherine Mowry LaCugna (San Francisco: HarperSanFrancisco, 1993), 126. "If in a patriarchal culture a woman had preached compassionate love and enacted a style of authority that serves, she would most certainly have been greeted with a colossal shrug" (ibid.).

[34]It might have come as a surprise to Jesus' disciples when he first appeared to the women after the resurrection, just as it came as a surprise to them that he would take children seriously. The power of women in labor unions is equally surprising for many. See, for instance, Mary Margaret Fonow, *Union Women: Forging Feminism in the United Steelworkers of America* (Minneapolis: University of Minnesota Press, 2003).

[35]Yates, *Why Unions Matter,* 155.

[36]Ibid., 162.

[37]Helene Slessarev-Jamir, *Prophetic Activism: Progressive Religious Justice Movements in Contemporary America* (New York: New York University Press, 2011), 118.

[38]Benjamin Robinson, "Can the Colonial Order Be Redeemed: Fanon and the Politics of 'Burning it Down,'" term paper, Southern Methodist University, December 2014.

Chapter 4: Labor Radicalizing Religion

[1]Lydia Saad, "Americans' Support for Labor Unions Continues to Recover," August 17, 2015. Gallup Poll, http://www.gallup.com/poll/184622/americans-support-labor-unions-continues-recover.aspx.

[2]Ken Fones-Wolf, *Trade Union Gospel: Christianity and Labor in Industrial Philadelphia 1865–1915* (Philadelphia: Temple University Press, 1989), describes the interactions of religion and labor in late nineteenth and early twentieth-century Philadelphia. Trade unions and religious leaders were able to learn from each other. The author concludes, "The interaction of churches and organized labor transformed both sides" (ibid., 192).

[3]The term *ultimate concern* was coined by theologian Paul Tillich.

[4]Most of the references are found in the Psalms, which is probably why so many people are familiar with the notion of God as king. The apostle Paul, on the other hand, never refers to God as king.

[5]See, for instance, Samuel 8:11–18. In Samuel 8:7, God seems to be opposed to giving the people a king because this means that they are rejecting God as their king. However, the kings on earth are very different kinds of kings than God, as they tend to exploit and oppress the people.

[6]Robert Anthony Bruno, *Justified by Work: Identity and the Meaning of Faith in Chicago's Working-Class Churches* (Columbus: Ohio State University Press, 2008), 223. Bruno claims that working people are also more susceptible to religious fraud (ibid., 225).

[7]See, for instance, the Babylonian creation mythos *Enuma Elish,* which shares certain parallels with the biblical accounts.

[8]See, for instance, the Nicene Creed of 325 CE and the Chalcedonian Confession of 451 CE See also Joerg's interpretations of these traditions in Joerg Rieger, *Christ and Empire: From Paul to Postcolonial Times* (Minneapolis: Fortress Press, 2007), chap. 2.

[9]This modern understanding of religion is increasingly being deconstructed in the contemporary study of religion. See, for instance, Tomoko Masuzawa, *The Invention of the World Religions: Or, How European Universalism Was Preserved in the Language of Pluralism* (Chicago: The University of Chicago Press, 2005).

[10]See, for instance, the work of the Buddhist Peace Fellowship; http://www.buddhistpeacefellowship.org.

[11]This is one of the key insights of the various theologies of liberation.

[12]For more succinct reflections on class see Joerg Rieger, ed., *Religion, Theology, and Class: Fresh Engagements after Long Silence* (New York: Palgrave Macmillan, 2013).

[13]See Frederick Herzog, *Justice Church: The New Function of the Church in North American Christianity* (Maryknoll, NY: Orbis Books, 1980).

[14]The German sociologist Max Weber has analyzed the legacy of Protestantism in particular as it relates to the development of capitalism.

[15]This is the literal meaning of the Hebrew word *shub*, which in theology is often linked to acts of repentance and conversion.

[16]For the history, see Kevin M. Kruse, *One Nation Under God: How Corporate America Invented Christian America* (New York: Basic Books, 2015).

[17]E. J. Dionne Jr., William A Galston, Korin Davis, Ross Tilchin, *Faith in Equality: Economic Justice and the Future of Religious Progressives* (Washington, DC: Governance Studies at Brookings, 2014), 49, http://www.brookings.edu/~/media/research/files/reports/2014/04/24-faith-in-equality/brookingsfaithinequalityfinal-%284%29.pdf.

[18]Ibid., 50.

[19]Ibid., 26.

[20]See the monumental biography by Eberhard Bethge, *Dietrich Bonhoeffer: A Biography*, trans. Eric Mosbacher et al. (Minneapolis: Fortress Press, 2000).

[21]Investigating this matter is one of the interests of Joerg's research. From a different perspective, see also James W. Perkinson, *Messianism against Christology: Resistance Movements, Folk Arts, and Empire*, New Approaches to Religion and Power (New York: Palgrave Macmillan, 2013).

[22]See Albert Raboteau, *Slave Religion: The "Invisible Institution" in the Antebellum South* (New York: Oxford University Press, 1978). Recall that the Nation of Islam was founded in 1930s, still under the impression of the ongoing struggles of African Americans.

[23]Part of this history is described by Fones-Wolf, *Trade Union Gospel.* Fones-Wolf comments that "because Protestants still hoped to speak for the majority of the population, they had to offer some comfort for the working class" (ibid., 197).

[24]For references to particular documents see the next chapter.

[25]This has happened before. Heath Carter, *Union Made: Working People and the Rise of Social Christianity in Chicago* (Oxford: Oxford University Press, 2015), has recovered the history of the early Social Gospel movement, which was shaped by working people. Only later did professional ministers and theologians follow this lead.

[26]For a brief introduction of the history and the basic concerns and insights of these organizations, both founded in 1996, see Helene Slessarev-Jamir, *Prophetic Activism: Progressive Religious Justice Movements in Contemporary America* (New York: New York University Press, 2011), 97–130. Differences in organizing include a stronger focus on clergy participation with IWJ compared to a stronger focus on local congregations with CLUE. In addition, while both

organizations take faith and religion seriously, CLUE puts stronger emphasis on what has been called "faith rooted" organizing. This kind of organizing is at the heart of Alexia Salvatierra and Peter Goodwin Heltzel, *Faith-Rooted Organizing: Mobilizing the Church in Service to the World* (Downers Grove, IL: Intervarsity Press, 2014). Salvatierra was a former director of CLUE and one of its founders.

[27]In the field of religious studies, tendencies to declare essential sameness were in fashion in the past. Today, there is broad agreement that such declarations were too superficial and are not desirable.

[28]While some of this is already happening in various ways, the practices of religious communities and the study of religion still have a great deal to learn here.

[29]Hamid Dabashi, *Islamic Liberation Theology: Resisting the Empire* (London: Routledge, 2008), 16, points out that what moves this new approach is not a universal idea of Islam—"rich Muslims of the Saudi family type" are not part of this movement—they rather seek to crush it while "poor and disenfranchised Americans, of the sort whose dead bodies were floating in the streets of New Orleans" are allies. This becomes especially meaningful as the spread of Islam globally is connected to "massive labor migrations," made worse by US-led wars against Muslim countries (ibid., 215, 217).

[30]This is the danger, for instance, of the argument of Samuel P. Huntington, *The Clash of Civilizations and the Remaking of World Order* (New York: Simon and Schuster, 1996).

[31]See the argument in Joerg Rieger and Kwok Pui-lan, *Occupy Religion: Theology of the Multitude*, Religion in the Modern World (Harrisburg, Pa.: Rowman and Littlefield, 2012).

[32]Hamid Dabashi, *Islamic Liberation Theology: Resisting the Empire* (London: Routledge, 2008), 232–33, talks about Islam as becoming a religion-in-the-world that interacts with other religions in the world—rather than being world religions; this requires dealing with grass roots movements in a cosmopolitan context.

Chapter 5: Religion Radicalizing Labor

[1]See, for instance, the lists of the prophets and their professions on the following website: http://www.questionsonislam.com/question/what-are-professions-prophets-mentioned-qur%E2%80%99.

[2]"When people experience sociopsychological strain, but lack the cultural or theological resources to make sense of it, they turn to the predominant ideology." Karen L. Bloomquist, *The Dream Betrayed: Religious Challenge of the Working Class* (Minneapolis: Fortress Press, 1990), 47.

[3]See, for instance, the reports of various Labor Seders since 2009, organized by the Washington, D.C.-based organization Jews United for Justice (http://jufj.org/content/labor-seder) that are now also augmented by a Social Justice Seder and a Racial Justice Seder.

[4]See the concerns expressed in the Jewish Labor Committee Passover Haggadah, Third Edition: Spring 2002, https://org2.salsalabs.com/o/5483/images/onlinehaggadah2014.pdf.

[5]See the excellent article of K.J. Noh, "The Economic Myths of Santa Claus," *Counterpunch*, December 25, 2014, http://www.counterpunch.org/2014/12/25/the-economic-myths-of-santa-claus/.

[6]Tariq Ramadan, *Radical Reform: Islamic Ethics and Liberation* (Oxford: Oxford University Press, 2009), 239. Without deeper resistance, the author argues, capitalism can easily coopt religion, including Islam (ibid., 244).

[7]C. Melissa Snarr, *All You That Labor: Religion and Ethics in the Living Wage Movement*, Religion and Social Transformation (New York: New York University Press, 2011), 156, emphasis in original.

[8]Rituals are also crucial in the work of Clergy and Laity United for Economic Justice (CLUE); see Slessarev-Jamir, *Prophetic Activism*, 111–12, and Salvatierra and Heltzel, *Faith-Based Organizing*.

[9]That working people identify religion with charity, with little awareness of the demands of justice, is also the conclusion of a study of Chicago's working-class churches by Robert Anthony Bruno, *Justified by Work: Identity and the Meaning of Faith in Chicago's Working-Class Churches* (Columbus: Ohio State University Press, 2008), 219–20.

[10]See Asghar Ali Engineer, The Prophet of Non-Violence: Spirit of Peace, Compassion, and Universality in Islam (New Delhi, Vitasta, 2011), 110.

[11]Friedrich A. von Hayek, *The Fatal Conceit: The Errors of Socialism*, ed. W. W. Bartley (Chicago: University of Chicago Press, 1988), 116–17.

[12]Chapter 11 of the NAFTA agreements even allows corporations to sue the governments of Canada, the United States, and Mexico for compensation if any of their policy decisions have a negative impact on their investments. See the *North American Free Trade Agreement*, "Chapter Eleven: Investments," http://www.sice.oas.org/trade/NAFTA/chap-111.asp.

[13]Aristotle noted the problem in his own way: "It is when equals have or are assigned unequal shares, or people who are not equal, equal shares, that quarrels and complaints break out." Aristotle, *Nicomachean Ethics*, trans. J. A. K. Thomson (New York: Penguin, 1955), V:III, 178.

[14]Farid Esack, *Qur'an, Liberation and Pluralism: An Islamic Perspective of Interreligious Solidarity against Oppression* (Oxford: OneWorld, 1997), 106.

[15]Most interpreters are now agreed on the centrality of the covenant and of relationship in the understanding of the biblical notions of justice. See, for example, Christopher D. Marshall, *Beyond Retribution: A New Testament Vision for Justice, Crime, and Punishment* (Grand Rapids, MI: Wm. B. Eerdmans, 2001); and Walter Kerber, Claus Westermann, and Bernhard Spörlein, "Gerechtigkeit," in *Christlicher Glaube in moderner Gessellschaft*, Teilband 17 (Freiburg: Herder, 1981).

[16]The verse ends: "And if it returns, then make settlement between them in justice and act justly. Indeed, Allah loves those who act justly." Qur'an 49:9. All quotations from the Qur'an are from the Sahih International Translation, which can also be found on the web at Quran.com.

[17]K. Koch, "sdq, gemeinschaftstreu/heilvoll sein," in *Theologisches Handwörterbuch zum Alten Testament*, vol. 2, ed. Ernst Jenni and Claus Westermann (Munich and Zurich: Christian Kaiser Verlag, Theologischer Verlag Zürich, 1984), 507–30.

[18]Dieter Lührmann, "Gerechtigkeit III," in *Theologische Realenzyklopädie*, vol. 12, ed. Gerhard Krause and Gerhard Müller (Berlin: Walter de Gruyter, 1984), 419. The New Testament use of the term differs from the classical Greek notion, which focuses exclusively on the relation between human beings.

[19]Esack, *Qur'an, Liberation and Pluralism,*103.

[20]Aryeh Cohen, *Justice in the City: An Argument from the Sources of Rabbinic Judaism* (Brighton, MA: Academic Studies Press, 2012), 120, 123.

[21]See Jewish theologian Moshe Weinfeld, "'Justice and Righteousness': The Expression and Its Meaning," in *Justice and Righteousness: Biblical Themes and Their Influence*, ed. Henning Graf Reventlow and Yair Hoffman (Sheffield: Sheffield Academic, 1992), 238. If space would permit, a narrative approach to biblical stories about God's justice would further demonstrate God's struggle to establish relationship in the face of broken relationships. Karen Lebacqz, *Justice in an Unjust World: Foundations for a Christian Approach to Justice* (Minneapolis: Augsburg Publishing House, 1987), works out such a narrative approach.

[22]See the examples in Weinfeld, "Justice and Righteousness," 242–43.

[23]This is the point of Elsa Tamez, *The Amnesty of Grace: Justification by Faith from a Latin American Perspective*, trans. Sharon Ringe (Nashville: Abingdon, 1993). Marshall, *Beyond Retribution*, 93, describes what Paul and the writers of

the gospels share in common: God's justice is "a redemptive power that breaks into situations of oppression or need in order to put right what is wrong and restore relationships to their proper condition."

[24]Gustavo Gutiérrez, *The Power of the Poor in History*, trans. Robert R. Barr (Maryknoll, NY: Orbis, 1983), 8, 10.

[25]This is one of the basic arguments of Joerg's book *God and the Excluded: Visions and Blindspots in Contemporary Theology* (Minneapolis: Fortress Press, 2001): inability to respect other human beings is related to the inability to respect God.

[26]See http://westandwiththe99percent.tumblr.com. Accessed October 8, 2015.

[27]The critique of idolatry is one of the central concerns of Marc Ellis, *Toward a Jewish Theology of Liberation: The Challenge of the Twenty-First Century*, 3rd edition (Waco: Baylor University Press, 2004), 163–76, 205, developed in conversation with Christian liberation theologies. This concern is seen as a bond between Jews and a link to other religious and humanist communities around the world.

[28]Dabashi, *Islamic Liberation Theology*, 254.

[29]Karl Barth, *Dogmatics in Outline* (New York: Harper and Row, 1959), 40, notes that the highness of God consists in God's descent into the "utter depths of the existence of his creature" in Jesus Christ.

[30]In the tenth century B.C.E. there was a budding metal industry on the Red Sea, supporting King Solomon's fleet. See Robert Banks, *God the Worker: Journeys into the Mind, Heart, and Imagination of God* (Eugene, OR: Wipf and Stock Publishers, 2008), 50. Several comparisons of God with a metal worker are found in the Hebrew Bible (e.g., Isa. 1:24–26; Ezek. 22:17–22; reference to God's work of purifying through fire).

[31]Banks, *God the Worker*, 58. A reference to the work of God's hands can be found in Psalm 95:5; Isaiah 64:8 provides a reference to God shaping the world and human beings. Jewish studies scholar Santiago Slabodsky tells us that this is not a very common interpretation with the Jewish rabbis, wondering whether the gender difference may be a reason.

[32]Banks, *God the Worker*, 87. God making garments is first referenced in Genesis 3:21, where God makes clothes for Adam and Eve. The metaphor of God making human beings is found in Job 10:10-12 and Psalm 139:13-16. According to Jesus in Matthew 6:30, God "clothes the grass of the field" and will also clothe human beings.

[33]Banks, *God the Worker*, 158. Ezekiel 36:36 talks about God replanting after a great destruction, visible to all nations. In Psalm 65:9–10, God is depicted as watering the earth. For the famous image of God as sower in the Gospels see Matthew 13:1–43; in verse 37, the sower is identified as the "Son of Man."

[34]Banks, *God the Worker*, 187, 189, notes that there were two kinds of shepherds: the herdsman who dwelled at the periphery of the city but was part of the economy, and the shepherd who was a nomad living in less inhabited areas. Both were marginal figures. In the Jewish Mishnah and Talmud shepherds are considered unclean, probably due to their inability to observe purity rites. The first reference to God as shepherd is found in Genesis 49:24. See also the famous Psalm 23. Jesus assumes images of the shepherd in the New Testament, for instance in John 10.

[35]Banks *God the Worker*, 219.

[36]For God as builder see Psalm 102:25; the reference is to construction work, not specialized. Other images include Psalm 104:3; Isaiah 40:12; Job 38:4–7; Proverbs 8:27–31. In Mark 6:3 and Matthew 13:55 Jesus is identified as carpenter.

[37]Khalil Ur Rehman, *The Concept of Labor in Islam* (Xlibris, 2010), 59; 60: "[Islam] tells the capitalist and the wealthy, that all they have is in due to their workers."

[38]Esack, *Qur'an, Liberation and Pluralism*, 106-7.
[39]Engineer, *The Prophet of Non-Violence*, 121.
[40]Ibid., 113.
[41]Ali Asghar Engineer, *Islam: Restructuring Theology* (New Delhi: Vitasta Publishing, 2012), 128.
[42]"Was die Welt im Innersten zusammenhält." Johann Wolfgang von Goethe, *Faust*.
[43]For Buddhist resources on labor see, for instance, http://www.iwj.org/resources/buddhist.
[44]Ken Estey, *A New Protestant Labor Ethic at Work* (Cleveland: Pilgrim Press, 2002), 93–140, describes the differences between company and business unionism and a broader vision for the unions, informed by an alternative "Protestant work ethic" that includes protest of and resistance to the dominant system rather than accommodation. For a recent critique of the limits of collective bargaining and union contracts see Stanley Aronowitz, *The Death and Life of American Labor: Toward a New Workers' Movement* (London: Verso, 2014).
[45]Snarr, *All You Who Labor*, 151.
[46]A similar case might be made for the Occupy Movement as well; see Rieger and Kwok, *Occupy Religion*.
[47]C. Melissa Snarr, *All You That Labor: Religion and Ethics in the Living Wage Movement*, Religion and Social Transformation (New York: New York University Press, 2011), 151.

Chapter 6: Organizing and Building the Movement

[1]Janice Fine, *Worker Centers, Organizing Communities at the Edge of the Dream* (Ithaca: Cornell University Press, 2006), 51, describes the social justice infrastructure that is in place in many churches and enables relatively easy access to church members who might be interested in becoming active in worker rights issues.
[2]For a short history on Jobs with Justice see Eric Larson, ed., *Jobs with Justice: 25 Years, 25 Voices* (Oakland: PM Press, 2013) or go to www.jwj.org for more information about the organization.
[3]For the text of the JwJ Pledge go to https://actionnetwork.org/forms/sign-the-jobs-with-justice-pledge?&source=NAT_W_homepage.
[4]C. Melissa Snarr, *All You That Labor: Religion and Ethics in the Living Wage Movement* (New York: New York University Press, 2011), 150–53, points out that collective identity and agency is built in coalitional work. The living wage campaign is an example where strong coalitions between labor, faith and community groups have changed the nature of politics in many cities and municipalities.
[5]Ruth Milkman, Joshua Bloom, Victor Narro, ed., *Working for Justice: The L.A. Model of Organizing and Advocacy* (Ithaca: Cornell University Press, 2010), 13.
[6]An Economix Blog article by Robert Gebloff anf Shaila Dewan, "Measuring the Top 1% by Wealth, Not Income," *The New York Times*, January 17, 2012, looks at the wealth of the 1 percent and gives these numbers, http://economix.blogs.nytimes.com/2012/01/17/measuring-the-top-1-by-wealth-not-income/?_r=0.
[7]See Angela Monaghan's article "US Wealth Inequality–top 0.1% worth as much as bottom 90%," *The Guardian*, November 13, 2014, http://www.theguardian.com/business/2014/nov/13/us-wealth-inequality-top-01-worth-as-much-as-the-bottom-90.
[8]A New York Times poll in 2014 showed that only 64 percent of respondents believed in "the American dream." This is the lowest percentage in that past twenty some years. Andrew Ross Sorkin and Megan Thee-Brenan, "Many Feel the American Dream IS Out of Reach, Poll Shows," *The New York*

Times, December 10, 2014, http://dealbook.nytimes.com/2014/12/10/many-feel-the-american-dream-is-out-of-reach-poll-shows/?_r=1.

[9]Dan Clawson, *The Next Upsurge: Labor and the New Social Movements* (Ithaca: Cornell University Press, 2003), 48, sums it up nicely: "Solidarity by a large number of people—not just leaders, not just staff—is the most powerful force labor has available. If workers, family members, and community allies develop solidarity and are prepared to take risks and make commitments, there is no limit to what they can accomplish."

[10]For practical collaborations between religion and labor see, *A Worker Justice Reader: Essential Writings on Religion and Labor,* ed. Joy Heine and Cynthia Brooke (Maryknoll, N.Y.: Orbis Books, 2010). For practical suggestions of how religious leaders, unions and corporate leaders can engage with a labor dispute, see Darren Cushman Wood, *Blue Collar Jesus: How Christianity Supports Workers' Rights* (Santa Ana, CA: Seven Locks Press, 2004), 170–74.

[11]William Barber II, with Barbara Zelter, *Forward Together: A Moral Message for the Nation* (St. Louis: Chalice Press, 2014), 158ff, states that because people across the South are experiencing the effects of income inequality and political polarization they are ready to mobilize and take action. Reverend Barber and the Forward Together Moral Movement have demonstrated that transformative relationships lead to actions for change.

[12]See also the WRB blog at http://wrbdallas.blogspot.com and the Facebook page of North Texas Jobs with Justice at https://www.facebook.com/jobs.withjustice.5. Both accessed October 9, 2015.

[13]Some of these are published in her recent hymnal: Jann Aldredge-Clanton and Larry E. Schultz, *Earth Transformed with Music! Inclusive Songs for Worship* (Woodway, TX: Eakin Press, 2015).

[14]For an interesting read of the life of a labor activist see Stewart Acuff, *Playing Bigger Than You Are: A Life in Organizing* (Minneapolis: Levins Publishing, 2012), and for an overview of the global struggle against neoliberalism see Notes from Nowhere, ed., *We Are Everywhere; The Irresistible Rise of Global Anticapitalism* (New York: Verso, 2003).

[15]Alexia Salvatierra was the director of CLUE California for many years. See Alexia Salvatierra and Peter Goodwin Heltzel, *Faith-Rooted Organizing: Mobilizing the Church in Service to the World* (Downers Grove, IL: InterVarsity, 2014)

[16]According to *Forbes Magazine,* Walmart is ranked no. 1 on the list of the world's five hundred largest companies with the highest total revenue for 2015. The company profiles are available on the web: http://fortune.com/fortune500/walmart-1/.

[17]"Work Matters to God" is the title of a sermon in a series of three sermons preached by Pastor Keith Stewart in response to his work with the Walmart Chaplains. See http://www.springcreekchurch.org/media.php?pageID=5 for a web link to the audio file. Accessed October 9, 2015.

[18]For a great resource on the basics of organizing see Kim Bobo, Jackie Kendall, and Steve Max, *Organizing for Social Change: Midwest Academy Manual for Activists* (Santa Ana, CA: Forum, 2010).

[19]For an example of churches, clergy, organizers and unions working together read about the Stamford Organizing Project in Dan Clawson, *The Next Upsurge–Labor and the New Social Movements* (Ithaca: Cornell University, 2003), 118–124.

[20]The police initially refused to arrest George Zimmerman, the security guard who shot Trayvon Martin who claimed self-defense, based on this gun lobby and ALEC-backed law. See the article by Sean Sullivan, "Everything you need to know about 'stand your ground' laws," *The Washington Post,* July 15, 2013, http://www.washingtonpost.com/news/the-fix/wp/2013/07/15/everything-you-need-to-know-about-stand-your-ground-laws/.

[21]See the article of Justin Levitt, "A comprehensive investigation of voter impersonation finds 31 credible incidents out of one billion ballots cast, " *The Washington Post*, August 6, 2014, http://www.washingtonpost.com/ news/wonkblog/wp/2014/08/06/a-comprehensive-investigation-of-voter-impersonation-finds-31-credible-incidents-out-of-one-billion-ballots-cast/.

[22]For more ideas on how nonprofits can build long-lasting changes, see Incite! Women of Color Against Violence, ed., *The Revolution Will Not Be Funded: Beyond the Non-Profit Industrial Complex* (Cambridge: South End, 2007), 129-49.

[23]One nurse in Texas who was fired for supporting an organizing drive was rehired because it is illegal to fire workers for that reason. Later she was fired again because it is not illegal in Texas to fire workers for *no* reason.

[24]For more examples on how companies fight back with union-busters see Clawson, *The Next Upsurge*, 3–9, and in the following chapters the author picks up on various organizing examples and weaves in the various steps employers took to intimidate workers and undermine the unionization process.

[25]See Priscilla Murolo, A.B. Chitty, Joe Sacco, *From the Folks Who Brought You the Weekend: A Short, Illustrated History of Labor in the United States* (New York: The New Press, 2001), for a comprehensive summary of the struggles of the labor movement in the United States.

[26]See chap. 2.

[27]See Joerg's book *No Rising Tide: Theology, Economics, and the Future* (Minneapolis: Fortress Press, 2009).

Conclusions

[1]Even the national AFL-CIO has renewed its interest in communities and community organizing (Resolution 16 of Quadrennial Convention in 2013), as well as in collaborations with religion (in its so-called "Southern Strategy").

[2]The event on religion and labor at the "Wild Goose Festival" in 2014 exceeded the expectations of organizers, drawing three or four times more people than the venue was designed to hold.

Index

Carter, Heath, 163n25

charity, 3, 53, 55, 58–59, 65, 67, 86–87, 107, 109, 114, 165n9

Christianity, 3, 5–6, 14, 19, 27, 29, 46, 58, 60, 63, 73, 83–85, 88,
90–91, 93, 96–98, 103–4, 106–9, 111–13, 116–20, 125, 136,
152, 156n17, 157n29, 159n24, 160n9, 162n2, 163n13,
163n16, 163n25 165n17, 165n21, 166n27, 168n10

Christmas, 105–9

class, 1, 4, 57, 81, 103, 106, 123, 129, 153, 159n1, 160n2–8, 160n14,
161n24, 161n27, 163n12
middle-, 1, 16, 24, 40, 44, 53–54, 57, 60–62, 75–76, 80, 121, 148
ruling-, 57, 116, 118
struggle, 56, 64, 69, 87, 90, 161n23
working-, 1, 40, 57, 62, 106, 155n1, 158n8, 159n32, 162n6,
163n23, 164n2, 165n9

Clawson, Dan, 168n9, 168n19, 169n24

Clergy and Laity United for Economic Justice (CLUE), xi, 96, 149,
152, 163n26, 165n8, 168n15

coalition building, 47, 51, 99, 136, 140–42, 149, 167n4

Cohen, Aryeh, 112, 161n19, 165n20

collective bargaining, 27, 36–37, 94, 127, 144, 157n27, 158n9,
167n44

conversion, 65–66, 90–91, 163n15

Cowie, Jefferson, 160n5

culture, xii, 12, 16, 25, 98–99, 162n33

Dabashi, Hamid, 99, 164n29, 164n32, 166n28

Dallas, xiii, xv, 34, 38, 41–42, 46, 81, 95, 125–28, 131, 135–36, 141–
44, 146, 155n3, 157n2–3, 168n12

Day, Dorothy, 72, 162n30

Day-Lower, Donna C, 156n4

debt, 30–32, 61, 157n30

democracy, viii, 10, 15, 19, 32, 68, 142, 147, 152, 156n4

desire(s), 6, 19–20, 39, 92, 104

distribution, vii, viii, 18, 39, 51, 156n7

diversity, 2, 71, 76, 97

domination, 12

Draper, Jonathan, 161n20, 161n22

Du Bois, W.E.B., 71, 162n29

---

economics, xii, xiii, 9, 12, 16–18, 38, 68–69, 86, 88, 102, 105, 112,
114, 147, 152, 156n1, 156n7, 161n21, 161n25, 169n27

Ellis, Marc, 166n27

Encyclicals, Papal, 157n27

Engineer, Ali Asghar, 118, 165n10, 167n39, 167n41

Esack, Farid, 111, 118, 165n14, 165n19, 167n38

Estey, Ken, 50, 156n17, 159n34, 167n44